Wildflower Perennials for Your Garden

Wildflower Perennials for Your Garden

a detailed guide to years of bloom
from America's long-neglected native heritage

Bebe Miles

illustrated by H. Peter Loewer

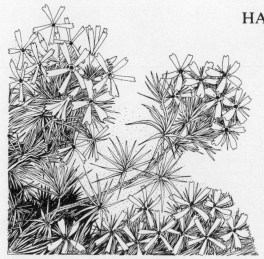

HAWTHORN BOOKS, INC.
Publishers / NEW YORK
A Howard & Wyndham Company

This book is affectionately and gratefully dedicated to Mrs. Lynwood R. Holmes who for more than forty years has devoted much of her life to the conservation of the flora of the northeastern United States.

Contents

PART II
100 Native American Perennials for Culture

Acknowledgments

I cannot possibly acknowledge all who have helped make this book possible. It is a distillation of more than forty years of watching wildflowers and of advice from many different sources over that period. I would, however, like to make special mention of Mrs. Emmitt Cartwright and David E. Benner, both of New Hope, Pennsylvania, and Oliver J. Stark of Newtown, Pennsylvania. They have been kind to answer questions and to share various facets of their own gardening experience. All have been associated with Bowman's Hill State Wildflower Preserve, Washington Crossing State Park, Washington Crossing, Pennsylvania. The great woman to whom this book is dedicated helped found that 100-acre sanctuary for our native plants. It has been a great schoolroom for many others besides me. The spot was set aside in 1934 as a living memorial to the patriots of Washington's army who camped among those hills on Christmas night before the famous crossing of the Delaware River and the decisive Battle of Trenton. What better way to commemorate those turbulent founding years than to come of age in our gardens—to make better use of this great botanical heritage of ours?

Wildflower Perennials for Your Garden

Introduction

If you like to garden, this book is for you. It is not a volume for the specialist in the exotic or the difficult; it is specifically written for the home gardener. I have selected the 100 best perennial mainland American plants that in my experience offer the most for garden use. Related species with garden possibilities are also briefly mentioned so that there are perhaps 500 or so additional native plants covered. With a few notable exceptions, these are the easiest members of the native flora to cultivate. They are also, in my opinion, the showiest or most useful for one reason or another.

Every wildflower enthusiast will find a personal favorite omitted. Some of mine have been, too, for one must draw many lines to select only 100 plants from the bewildering variety that grow wild somewhere from Maine to Florida, from Quebec to California and Washington. Availability was one criterion for selection. There are only two featured genera difficult to locate through dealers. (Both are so important and lovely they deserve wider attention, and I'm hoping this book will bring it to them.) The source list in the Appendix is as up-to-date as any you will find anywhere.

I readily admit there are many more northeastern plants included in this book than species from other parts of the United States or Canada. These are the plants I know best, of course, but even in western catalogs these are often the species offered. For one thing, they may be more adaptable than plants that come from a very local area in the northwestern mountains, the southwestern deserts, or the subtropical climate of the southeastern states. For another, the Creator was particularly kind in distributing plants in the great northeastern tier. The extremes in climate, topography, soil types, and even in the various kinds of primeval forest were more marked there, and a variety of plants evolved to fit all the different situations. Moreover, it is an older part of the United States in terms of recorded historical experience. Botanists have combed the Catskills, the Adirondacks, and the Appalachians much more thoroughly than the Sierra Nevadas, so we know more about the eastern flora. Many more people have been involved in appreciating it over a longer period of time. The west no doubt has plenty of good plants to offer, but so far these have fewer advocates or dealers willing to propagate them.

The 100 plants presented here are really only a jumping-off place for the dedicated gardener. This book is not intended to limit you to the 100 or even just to their near relatives. It should pique you to investigate further the great list of native plants—as well as fine garden inhabitants from other parts of the world. (Some good sources of further reading are listed in the Appendix.) There must be plants indigenous only to your own part of the country. That they are not listed here does not mean they are not garden-worthy. Indeed, we need far more trials of various American plants, and perhaps one day all our gardens will be the richer for your experimentation.

Purists may quarrel over my insistence that in some cases selections and hybrids are the better choices for the ordinary garden than the original species. That dissent makes no sense to me whatsoever. One might just as well insist that we throw away all the gorgeous hybrid daffodils and plant only the species, an action that would rob our gardens of much of their springtime gaiety.

One of the reasons why conservationists work so hard to preserve an individual species is because its demise diminishes the gene pool provided by a benificent nature. Once a particular species has died out (be it animal or plant), that is the end of the trail. Man can create hybrids, but he cannot bring a species into being. We have not shown so much intelligence in our dealings with the natural world that we can decide positively at any one point in history what may become important in the future. Only so short a time ago as in my own grandmother's girlhood the tomato was viewed with suspicion in many quarters. So the preservation of any species is important, and I am all for it. But part of the significance of a species is as a possible parent for a future hybrid, a plant usually stronger than either of its parents. As far as selections go, only a dimwit would refuse to acknowledge a plant with better flowers or growth habits than the type, and we don't need any more encouragement of mediocrity in our lives.

In a sense, to separate the plants available for our gardens into separate lists of "garden perennials" and "hardy wildflowers," as so many catalogs do, is a sign of our continued adolescence despite the Bicentennial. I suppose it was once done as a conservation measure to point up the importance of the natives. Now that we are of age, I hope the larger dealers will soon simply divide their offerings by habitat (sun, shade, moistness, etc.). Oddly enough, one catalog that does differentiate between perennials and wildflowers has let some twenty-one popular American genera stray into the section on hardy perennials! The beginning gardener thus fails to appreciate quite how much his garden actually may owe to the native influence.

Actually the word *wildflower* is a paradox to start with. Many species tulips are wildflowers in Turkey or Greece but treasured as garden delights in the rest of the world. If I were to point them out as wildflowers to visitors to my Pennsylvania garden, they would think me daft. Conversely, the bloodroot, which grows in open woods from eastern Canada to Florida and Texas, is described thusly in an English gardening book: "Although quite hardy, it also makes a good alpine house plant." The resident of Maine or Michigan who reads that laughs.

Obviously what is a wildflower depends on where your garden is. In my own garden during the season are regal lilies from the mountains of China, snowdrops from the Caucasus, caladiums from South America, and calla lilies from Africa—all of them wildflowers in their place of origin. This book just happens to be concentrating on perennials native to North America. As a group they are no more and no less difficult than wildflowers from any part of the world. What I hope you will learn is that our American plants have just as much to offer the gardener as do any imports *if they are grown under the proper conditions.* And that isn't an esoteric limitation either; no one successfully grows dahlias from Mexico in the shade, nor impatiens from Malaya in hot sun. The American perennials have an added attraction, in that once planted correctly, many will provide years of attractive garden decoration in our climate without much further work on your part. You could hardly say that about either the dahlias or the impatiens!

A few wildflower dealers are guilty of touting an introduced plant from Europe or Asia simply because it is found so often in today's fields or along roadsides. Star-of-Bethlehem, yellow marsh iris, the European celandine poppy, Deptford pink, butter-and-eggs, Queen Anne's-lace, teasel, and chicory (to name just a few of the most ubiquitous) are none of them native plants. None of them will ever become scarce, simply because they are so well adapted to living with civilized man. They started arriving here with the first colonists, often in horse or cattle fodder or with ballast stones. Some of them are pretty weedy, too.

If you have gathered from the foregoing that I am recommending the 100 genera described later in this book simply because they are American, you have missed the point. They are included here because they are excellent plants for various types of gardens. I rather hope this is the last time I shall write about them just because they are American. They are deservedly good perennials, and their point of origin would be unimportant if they had not been neglected by so many in the mainstream of American gardening.

For your convenience the selected genera have been divided into three sections: plants for sunny places, those for shady sites, and those that prosper only in wet spots. These three conditions have more influence on what can successfully grow where than any other limitations. On the introductory page for each of the three sections you will find additional plants for that type of environment, which are mentioned briefly under the "related species" heading of other entries. You can locate these through the Index.

A real attempt has been made to list all the popular names given to one of the featured species, and they are all entered in the Index for ready finding. Although the most common popular name is featured at the top of each page in the text, you will find that the listings in each section are alphabetical by botanical name. After much thought, this arrangement proved the only one that had merit. I started to list plants alphabetically by popular name and soon found that I myself could not remember under which nickname I had filed a particular species, for some of them have a good many common names. What is worse, some of the popular names overlap. There must be dozens of American plants called snakeroot in some locality. Rather makes you feel sorry for the unfortunate early settler who suffered snakebite.

At any rate, the botanical listings should make it easier to use this book for quick reference without constant turning to the Index. I don't know why as a gardening nation we should be so timid about using botanical names. They are the only way to be sure you are buying what you really want. Sometimes one of the audience at a lecture will come up to me afterward and comment admiringly on my use of botanical names. I don't know why it should be any harder to learn *Asclepias tuberosa* than pleurisy-root, especially when all of us go around saying aster, delphinium, and phlox, all three of which are botanical terms.

There is nothing mysterious about the system of botanical classification, which is termed binomial nomenclature. Using the flower and its parts as a basis, scientists have assigned each plant to a particular genus (plural: genera). Within each genus there may be closely related plants, and to differentiate between them each has a specific tag, just as people do. Thus there is *Viola pedata* (birdfoot violet) and *Viola pensylvanica* (smooth yellow violet). Both are violets, but they are very different in color, leaf shape, and habits. To obtain the exact violet you want in your garden, both you and the dealer must use the botanical names rather than popular nicknames, which differ from place to place.

The same generic and specific names are used all over the world, and it is a wonderfully handy way to keep straight the great host of plants God gave us. Usually botanical names are printed in italics. Where there is no chance of a mistake, they may be shortened, as *V. pedata*. Family classifications are interesting and sometimes give hints about flower shapes.

Having just assured you the names are the same, I must now

7

admit there is some ambiguity. The botanical rule is that the first person to describe a species has the right to name it. Sometimes later research turns up an earlier reference than had been subsequently credited. For that very reason our poor smooth yellow violet is still *V. eriocarpa* in some texts, although Asa Gray (our authority) lists *V. pensylvanica* as the preferred reference. Where I am aware an outdated binomial is still in use in some catalogs, I have listed it for convenience. Thankfully, this confusion does not occur often.

Perhaps it is fear of mispronouncing the botanical name that holds so many back. Let me tell you a secret. I learned to read at a very early age and was soon tearing through books filled with words that seldom entered ordinary conversations, especially those in the school playground. As I read, I made up my own pronunciations, and some of them are still there, lurking beneath my subconscious to trip me up on occasion. This has never prevented me from talking. So take the botanicals to your tongue and don't worry. The bastardized Latin and Greek used in botany can hardly afford to put on airs.

One more point needs emphasizing. We are considering perennials in this book. By definition that means a plant that lives over year after year. Those that are not evergreen will die down with frost, but new shoots will appear in the spring. Some plants included here are technically bulbs or tubers or rhizomes or thick underground stems. These are different botanically from a herbaceous perennial, which forms a mass of fibrous roots. But they all act the same in delivering a new crop of flowers and foliage every year; for our purposes they all accomplish the same thing in the garden.

Some perennials, however, tend to smother themselves after a few years by their own exuberance at increasing. Asters, tall summer phlox, and helenium are three such that come quickly to mind. Such plants are true perennials but need some attention from the gardener. If you notice that a plant is getting many offsets around the original or has established a very thick clump of shoots, it may well benefit from division. (This technique is described in detail in the chapter on propagation.) Division keeps a plant thrifty.

Mulching, watering in drought, and weeding are other tasks that may have to be done to keep a plant perennially growing well. True, such attentions do not take place in the wild, but there is a vast difference between a woodland, where it does not matter where a plant wanders or even if it survives, and a garden, where a certain placement of plants makes for optimum effect. It is not safe to think that you can simply plant a perennial and forget it, certainly not if you want it to do its utmost in your garden.

It would have been lovely to have illustrated all 100 of the selected species in full color, but with today's costs it would have put the price of this book beyond reasonable bounds. The brief description of height, color, and habitat for each plant should give you a good idea of whether it will make a worthwhile decorative for your individual needs. Peter Loewer's clever drawings are designed to give you a view of the physical form of both flower and plant. While the flowers are surely the first thing anyone thinks about, they are not always the most important factor in placing a plant in the garden. A species that has interesting foliage all season may offer more to the total picture than one with gorgeous but fleeting bloom. Ideally, a garden contains a blend of both, so that there are exciting flowers from time to time but a general aura of pleasant green during the rest of the growing year. The artist shows you how each plant looks in its mature growth.

PART I
Preparing Your Garden

1
Be Objective about Your Property

Your garden should reflect your color preferences, your flower favorites, and your lifestyle. Unfortunately, however, you must be objective about what you can do outdoors on a given piece of land. Indoors you can switch from modern to traditional just by buying new furniture, changing wallpapers and fabrics, or even by physically altering the sizes and shapes of rooms. Outdoors is another matter entirely. In gardening, you are limited by the environment. For example, whatever climate you live in has definite extremes of either cold or heat. The next chapter details ways in which you can stretch those limitations, but these manipulations can only go so far.

Just as important are several other factors which vitally affect what you can plant: amount of sun or shade available; amount of seasonable rainfall and whether your site sits high and dry or low and wet; soil fertility and type; and, finally, your available time and personal dedication to gardening.

The last factor may sound facetious. After all, why would you be reading this book if you were not interested in gardening? Nevertheless there are those for whom growing things is a pleasant adjunct to life, and there are others for whom it is an all-absorbing interest. This chapter is more important to the first group. The point is that if gardening is to be an enjoyable avocation, you must learn to get along with the natural world as it exists in your corner of it. The professional or the enthusiast may be willing to go to any trouble to make a particular plant happy. This book is not written for them. It assumes that most of you consider gardens only one part of your life. Some flowers for cutting, a pleasant setting for a home, an easy-to-care-for yard are what such gardeners seek. And such goals become much easier to attain if one takes a few moments to consider very objectively natural habitat factors before ordering plants.

The healthiest, hardiest plant will fade away if it is put into an environment for which it is not suited. A nature preserve may go to all kinds of trouble to provide the correct habitat for a desired plant. The casual gardener, however, should go at it the other way: what plants will do well under the given conditions? You need to consider your property as a series of possible habitats.

Is It Dry or Wet?

If your property or climate is very dry, you can by dint of some extra work and ingenuity make it somewhat wetter. You can't create a bog in the middle of the desert, or at least you ought not to try. But you can definitely mix plenty of humus into sandy soil to aid its water retention, and you can usually spare some water for the garden in drought; even if it means going to such extremes as diverting kitchen and bath water to the garden rather than the drains. Even in the desert you can create a small artificial pond if your psyche insists. Wherever you are making a wet-site garden, however, do give some thought to what happens when drought comes. If such a garden is located too far from a water source, you face future problems.

Many properties that are intrinsically dry have a wet spot: a low depression where rain collects, the area below a drain spout, or even a few square feet around a birdbath or a goldfish pond. There, one of the moisture-loving plants is a good choice.

Unfortunately, you cannot change a wet situation into a dry one as easily as dragging out the hose solves a drought. You can improve drainage somewhat, but it is an expensive proposition. It involves drain fields, diversion ditches, and possibly even large earthmoving machines. If your property sits low in bottomland or flood plain, or if your water table is just below the surface in the garden area, you are wiser to concentrate on a garden that

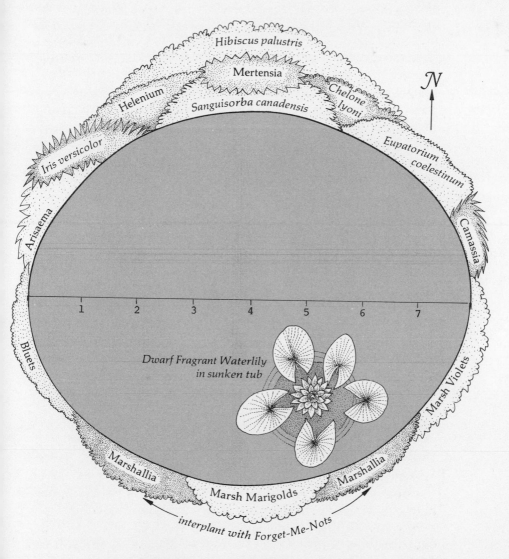

A Small Poolside Garden

Many excellent native perennials like their feet wet. In a miniature pond like this, a small tub for the water lilies would be easy to lift out if the pool is too shallow to keep the lilies immersed through the winter. Two small tubs close together can give an effect comparable to that obtained by using one large tub.

features plants that like it wet. On a small scale you can fashion a raised garden area that has better drainage by terracing or creating a small artificial hill. Low-lying land remains a wet spot and can even be subject to flooding. So if your garden is in such a spot, be grateful that there are plants which over the ages have evolved to live in such conditions. The section on plants that prefer wet feet is for you. Not only will they bring color and pleasure, but they will help hold the soil and prevent the erosion that inevitably occurs when water runs over soft earth.

A brook wandering through a property can be a real delight. It opens up all sorts of gardening possibilities. Marsh or bog areas can be somewhat tamed, too, if you have time and money at hand. Such places develop naturally where there is a low spot and poor drainage. I have a neighbor who created a large pond where geese and ducks congregate to entertain us all. It had been marsh before, and it required earthmoving equipment, engineers, and lots of money to turn it into open water. Stocked with fish to eat mosquito larvae, it is certainly nicer to live near than the marsh it replaced. It remains, however, a wet environment. The trees and shrubs and smaller plants that occupy its verge are those which revel in moisture, and that's as it should be.

How Much Sunshine or Shade Do You Have?

Sunshine is another variable. If you move into a tract house where the developer has chopped down every tree (and damn him to eternity) or if your property was formerly cleared farmland, you need not mourn forever the lack of shade. Start planting trees immediately. (If you are in such a position, do read the section on planning before you plunge into an orgy of planting.) You'll want some fast growers for quick protection from the sun, but the amazing thing is to see what any properly planted tree can do in five years. Even the smallest bush casts some shade on its northern side, so all is not lost if your heart yearns for a woodland garden. Remember, you do not need a forest to create such a spot. One or two trees will provide a mini-woodland on the smallest lot. It will take a bit longer than if the trees were there in the beginning, but eventually you will have your shady garden. It may even be a

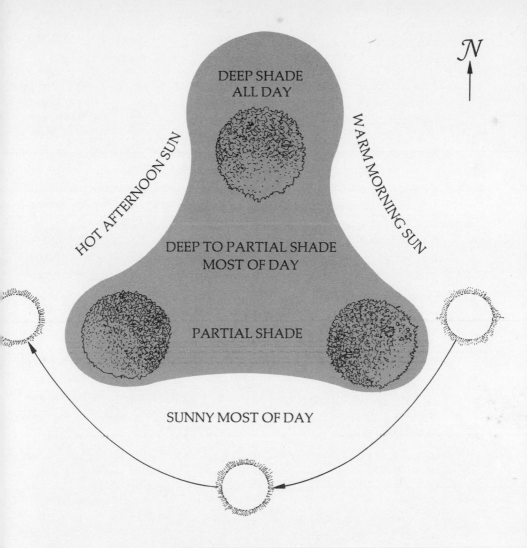

Varying Shade Zones

With only three trees planted in a triangle, you can create a miniature woodland with several varying shade zones.

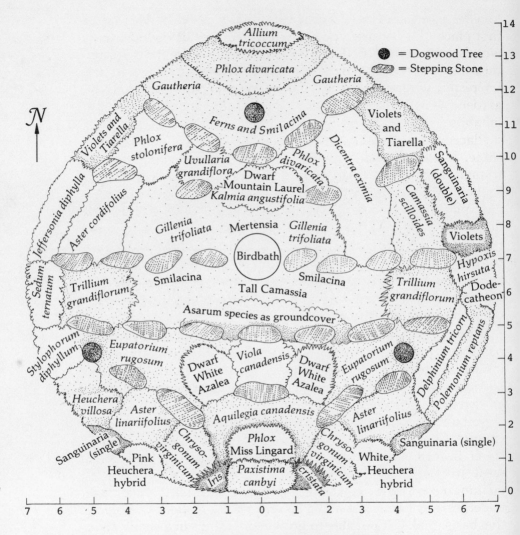

A Miniature Woodland Garden

Even on a small property you can simulate a flowering woodland. If space permits, the three trees indicated in this garden plan can be planted farther apart. The lower branches of dogwoods should be trimmed to allow more light and provide maximum ground space for small plants. Stepping stones enable you to get in to work; they will not be particularly noticeable. Violas, primroses, endymion, and many other shade-loving plants would also be quite at home in a habitat like this.

lovelier spot than if you had trees naturally growing there in the first place, this because you can select trees like dogwoods, sourwoods, and stewartias. These types give extra decoration because they have flowers at some period of the year, good fall color, and interesting winter silhouettes. They make a much more intriguing garden than the maples, oaks, and ashes that are more common inhabitants of the woodland.

Placement and species of trees also effects the amount of sunshine. In the woodland garden on page 18, for example, if the triangle is reversed so that there are two trees to the north and one to the south, the resulting garden will have considerably more sun and plant selection will vary accordingly. I have indicated dogwoods simply because they are such a wonderful small garden tree and because their habit of growing horizontal branches makes for quick shade. You can substitute other small trees, but check their growth habits first. Slender birches cast much less shade. A vigorous crabapple will cast much more and requires more space than a dogwood for branching.

If you already live in the woods, a sunny garden may not be possible. Chopping down full-grown trees is not only a big undertaking but rather a radical step merely to enable you to have one particular kind of garden. It would make more sense to tailor the garden to the prevailing conditions.

You can do some selective trimming, however, which may well enlarge the scope of your shady garden. Some trees can have their lower branches pruned off to let more light in. Perhaps some scrub trees or excess saplings should be cut down to give the remaining trees better light and air, and, incidentally, encourage undergrowing plants. Cleaning up underbrush, if done on a selective basis, makes it possible to grow more things in a shady area. Learn the names and habits of the shrubs and trees you have before going at any job like this. Native rhododendrons, flowering trees, blueberries, and ferns will add to the effectiveness of a shady garden. Chokecherry, poison ivy, catbrier, and rampant honeysuckle are well worth eliminating. Those who already have an existing woodland can make it a magic place by adding colonies of some of the showy flowers in the shady plant section. Such an area is as truly a garden as any sunny border.

Shade comes in many forms. Almost nothing will grow in the

darkness of the middle of a mature stand of evergreens. You can use them, however, as an excellent all-year windbreak and as background for a garden on the sunnier fringes. Seen from a distance, the foamy white of springtime shadbush, the chaste chalices of the summertime franklinia tree, or the late season fire of the winterberry show up much better against the green of pines and hemlocks.

Deciduous trees, on the other hand, cast a different kind of shadow. If the trees are tall with few lower branches, much sunlight seeps into that area during the first months of the growing season. Here plants with short, early spring lives will do very well. If the trees are not too close together, there will be filtered sunlight even during the summer, and this changing pattern of light and dark suits many woodland plants even better than constant shade. Finally, a garden around a tree has fringe areas that get sunshine in morning or afternoon, and those few hours of extra light will further expand what plants you can easily introduce successfully.

You will find plants in the section for shady gardens that need or will do well in only partial shade, and you will find others in the sunny garden section that will tolerate some shade. So the number of different plants you can grow on a property with trees is greater than might seem possible at first glance.

What about Soil?

Within certain limitations you can do something about the tilth—cultivation quality—of your soil. When we bought our current house, we thought the land was former fertile Bucks County farmland. Only later did we discover the topsoil had all been scraped off, and our "garden" was nothing but clay and rocky silt. When I say clay, I mean a nasty tight kind of soil that bakes hard in summer, stays wet late into spring, and drains only very slowly. Long ago we lost count of how many bags and bales of peat moss we have mixed into that hardpan as we planted and cultivated. Untold quantities of shredded bark mulch were purchased and spread, too. We have gathered bushels of leaves from luckier neighbors and dragged them uphill to dig into the fallow winter garden. We have made compost and buried garbage, dug in green cover crops, and begged leafmold from generous friends. Slowly we have changed that stubborn clay into garden loam. It has been backbreaking labor sometimes. One of my friends complains that her land is too sandy, that it drains too well. She has had to do some of the same things we did to add humus to her soil, but her battle has been easier than our campaign against the clay.

So even if you don't have the soft, friable garden or woods loam that is ideal, you need not give up hope. Start improving one small spot for the first garden and persevere. It is hard to add too much humus to any soil, and all gardeners should be constantly replenishing it by one means or another. Nature lends a helping hand too. The baby trees we planted with so much labor are now large enough to drop leaves to help us, and because we have composted in place under some of them, we have a spot that begins to resemble a woodland both in tree canopy and decent soil. Many of the plants that prefer a woodsy situation do not put down great root systems if the top six inches of soil is to their liking. So we are not talking about major excavations except in the case of planting trees.

You may not have to go to quite so much trouble to make your gardens. With even halfway decent soil, you can accomplish a great deal simply by adding some peat moss to the soil every time you plant. Add a mulch (see pages 23–26) and the greatest number of plants will do nicely.

One thing about soil that can give you some fairly permanent problems is acidity or alkalinity. This is measured by a pH reading. A pH of 7 is neutral. Lower numbers indicate acidity, higher ones alkalinity. The only tricky part is to remember that each number gradation represents a multiple of 10, so that soil with a pH of 6 is 10 times more acid than pH 7, and one with a pH of 5 is 100 times more acid than neutral soil. By far the greatest number of plants in this book grow best in soil around pH 6. The black Michigan and Pennsylvania peat moss we buy in bags tests out around that figure, while the rough sphagnum peat from Canada sold in bales is somewhat more acid. Soil where oaks or pines have been dropping foliage over many years may easily test out around pH 5; soil in a natural sphagnum bog may go to pH 4. Farmers often add lime to their acres to sweeten the soil because many crops do best in soils close to neutral, but the plants in this book are not lime lovers for the most part.

In the northeast at least, chances are your soil is more acid than alkaline, but there are limestone areas. If you are in doubt, buy an inexpensive soil-testing kit. Try samples of your soil in various places and both at surface level and several inches beneath. Usually the top layer is more acid. Adding humus and peat moss as you plant will enable you to grow the greatest percentage of native Americans unless your soil is highly alkaline to start with.

What do you do if your soil is at one extreme or another? You can lessen the acidity by adding some lime, and you can lessen alkalinity by adding sphagnum peat, but the changes may be only temporary. What makes more sense is to concentrate on plants that prefer what you have. Above all, don't try very acid-loving plants like trailing arbutus if you have limy soil, and vice versa. Those whose soil has very high pH readings will find that many western plants from the Plains states are better choices, since soils in some of those states are alkaline.

Most of you will find your soil is around pH 6. For those few eastern plants that prefer a touch of lime, I have found that a mulch of marble chips seems to do wonders in my slightly acid soil. It lasts a long time, and the water from rain and snow slowly dissolves the chips to keep the plants happy with a drink of lime.

You need to remember that your water supply can have some effect, too. Our well water is quite acid and does terrible things to the plumbing fixtures, but it has a fine effect on most of our growing things. City water may be more nearly neutral but sometimes is quite alkaline. To hose really acid-loving plants like the arbutus with such water is to sicken them.

All this may sound more complicated than it is. Only a few of the plants included in the 100 species have very special needs. You can assume if there is no particular mention made of soil acidity that an individual species will do well in either neutral or slightly acid soil (the pH 6 that is fairly common in humusy loam). Plants preferring slightly acid reactions obviously are fine there, too. Where there is more stress on acidity, we are talking about a pH range going toward 5, and you may have to work at it. Very acid soil is close to pH 4, and it cannot be maintained in the ordinary garden without more trouble than it is worth. I do not suggest plants requiring that acid a soil for cultivation unless you already have soil naturally close to that level pH.

In the vital statistics for each featured species is the heading *Habitat.* I have tried to translate botanical descriptions into garden habitats to make it easier for you. Loam means good friable garden soil. Humusy soil means the addition of peat moss, etc., to bring garden soil closer to a woodland type of soil, which is very porous but in its topmost inches is full of humus from decaying leaves and wood. The presence of adequate humus in the soil is far more important than adding fertilizers. Small weak applications of food will not harm these plants, however. A thin soil, where that is indicated, is one with rock or gravel content or a sandy soil, and there is seldom much humus.

Human nature being what it is, we are always trying to create what we don't have. If you must grow a plant that needs soil quite different from what you have, here are a few pointers. Locate such a spot higher than the surrounding garden so that groundwater will not frustrate your attempt. Make a special soil mix for whatever condition you are after. Try to keep the soil from mixing with the rest of the area. At Bowman's Hill we have used old bathtubs and coffin covers to frustrate wandering earthworms and seepage. You could line the bottom of such a spot with heavy plastic and make a slight wall of rocks or bricks. Such an elevated site will tend to dry out faster in drought but may not always drain well. Always mulch with some material that adds to the soil reaction in the direction at which you're aiming. Marble chips and wood ashes add lime. Cottonseed meal and pine needles are extra acid mulches. Obviously it is easier to devote most of your garden space to plants that want what you have.

Mulching

Nature abhors a vacuum. If you do not have a thick stand of grass in the lawn, weed seeds will find the bare spots. So too in the garden. Bare earth will not stay that way. Unless your plants are close enough together to cover the soil surface completely, something else will put down its roots too. Close planting is, therefore, a fine idea, but no garden is static. One plant outgrows its designated spot, another dies. And the weed seeds are always with us. To cut down the time spent in pulling out the undesirables, mulch the soil to make it harder for weeds to germinate and prosper. They will still enter, but in lesser quantities, and they will be easier to pull out.

Your garden plants will benefit in two ways. First, they will not need to compete with the weeds for available sun, food, and water. Second, the mulch will substitute neatly for what the plant roots get normally in nature. In the wild, the roots of woodland plants are protected by a layer of fallen leaves and leafmold, those in open situations by a thick turf of grass leaves in all stages of decay as well as the living blades. By spreading a mulch on the ground around your garden plants, you more nearly approach natural conditions. This top dressing keeps the plant roots cooler in summer and warmer in winter.

Most easily obtained mulches are organic. As they break down, they add more of that good humus to the soil. You can sweep away the mulch temporarily when planting or moving the inhabitants of the garden, but some of it is bound to be mixed back into the disturbed soil, and this, too, helps improve it.

For most gardens a mulch layer about an inch thick is quite enough. In a woodland garden, leaf drop will aid you immensely, and no mulch may ever be necessary if you encourage the leaves to pile up. In a small shady garden you can aid the process by raking all fallen leaves into the garden and holding them down against the winter winds with odd branches. As the leaves decay, they manufacture a fluffy black duff to cover the soil. But in the open garden, you will have to check your mulches every few years or so, for mulching is not a one-time operation. The easy way is to mulch as you plant initially, then add from time to time where the mulch has grown thin.

What to use as a mulch depends somewhat on where you live. It makes sense to use material that is cheap and easily obtained. The one thing you should not do is mulch with peat moss. Any kind of peat is a wonderful soil conditioner. Mixed thoroughly in the garden earth or in a potting medium, it helps retain moisture and encourages good root development. On the top of the soil, however, it can make an impenetrable crust, keeping out both air and moisture from the soil below. When it rains, a thick peat covering will absorb the water and actually rob the roots below of any at all.

A good mulch will let both moisture and air penetrate. The shredded pine bark available in handy bags at many supermarkets and virtually every garden center is one of the best and quite reasonable. You might find in your area buckwheat hulls, tobacco stems, chopped corncobs, tanbark, spoiled hay, marsh hay, bark nuggets, cocoa hulls, or some other organic waste material that is being recycled. The primary precaution is to make sure the material is not so light it will blow away. Weed-seed content and possible contamination from disease or bacteria of some sort are other factors to consider.

You can make great mulch yourself with a home shredder. Running the lawn mower over piles of leaves creates a nice free mulch, too, and it is less likely to blow away than full-sized leaves. Compost is always scarce but a great top dressing for gardens if you can spare it. Leafmold can be purchased but is expensive and perhaps best used for potting or very special areas.

Pine-needle mulch is sometimes sold or can be raked up where there are large stands of mature trees. Save it for plants wanting real acidity. Its porosity is legendary, and it lasts a long time.

Hereabouts we use pulled weeds and dried grass clippings to mulch areas where appearance is not too important. They have been piled for years under the small trees where we envision a new shady garden soon. Thick layers of newspaper weighted down with stones or a thin layer of soil are fine for keeping paths weed free, but appearance is a problem. Where you are intending to make a garden, a very thick layer of newspapers can be laid down a month before to kill the existing herbiage and make your initial digging a bit easier. So far those are the only ways to recycle paper in the garden that I have found satisfactory.

Rocks act as mulches, too. Alpine plants especially love to get their roots under boulders or gravel washes, where it is cooler and there may be more moisture. You can plant a garden area with something like columbines, which seem to like rocks as companions, and then place some rocks between the plants. If you don't have any big rocks, even small stones can be piled a few inches high in such a spot and camouflaged with some pine bark until the plants fill in.

Many different materials can be utilized as a mulch in the garden. Even other plants can be used this way. Overplanting a patch of Canada lilies with the creeping *Phlox divaricata* or a trillium bed with wild ginger helps to mulch the bulbs and tubers below as well as cover the bare soil around the other higher plants.

What about Pests and Diseases?

Another thing you have to consider about your property is its proximity to wild life. Four-footed pests can wreak real havoc in a garden. Mice and rats eat bulbs and tubers, rabbits will leave lettuce alone to dine on phlox, and deer relish a wide variety of plants. In theory these pests cause the most damage in parts of the property away from the house where it is easier for hungry animals to eat at leisure. But I have mice near the bird feeders, and rabbits often set up housekeeping in the shrubbery under the windows.

I have not found any chemical to work very well against any of these pests. Good garden cleanup helps discourage mice and rats, but there are times when poison is the only solution. Make sure you locate it under a board or poke it into the runs so birds and domestic animals cannot get at it. Incorporating gravel into the soil or mulching well with gravel above bulb beds discourages mice quite a lot.

Moles do no real damage, but their runs make it easy for mice to get to roots and bulbs. An old-fashioned spring trap works quite well against moles if set in a well-traveled tunnel.

A gun is a wonderful rabbit deterrent, but it is not always legal or wise. The rabbits are so prolific hereabouts that I must fence the entire vegetable garden. In my flower gardens I fashion cylinders of chicken wire one or two feet high and anchor them with sticks to protect certain very attractive plants like phlox. These devices are not very noticeable, especially during the summer when the plants are in good growth. Without them I could not grow certain plants at all. Branches of needled evergreens also seem to discourage rabbits. I arrange them during the lean days of winter and spring in circles around crocus and other tempting delicacies.

Deer have proliferated far too well in many areas of suburbia. With much land posted against hunting and laws against shooting near human habitations, the herds have become a real menace to the gardener who lives beyond thickly settled sections. One of my neighbors recently counted a herd of eighteen.

Fencing is one way to discourage deer, albeit expensive. Sometimes, however, it does not seem to take much fence to detour them. I have one friend who simply strings a wire at breast height from tree to tree at the back of her place where the deer enter. She ties white rags to the wire at intervals and reports it has worked quite well. Another ingenious botanist I know strung the wire the same way at the back of his property, then hung old sections of clattering venetian blinds at intervals. That worked, too. Everything else failing, you may have to site your garden closer to the house or limit the plants in outlying sections to genera deer do not like.

One of the worst pests here is the slug. This slimy relative of the snail may not look dangerous, but its appetite for green things is astounding. It usually prefers the succulent new growth on your rarer treasures. Slugs eat at night and delight in damp situations. The humusy soil and mulch suggested for so many of the plants in these pages provide slugs especially attractive homesites. And underneath rocks, logs, birdbath stands, and sidewalks slugs lay their eggs and rest during hot sunny hours. A shake of salt will kill a slug; but if you have many, you can hardly dent the population that way. Besides, concentrated salt is not good for plants. The highly touted open saucers of stale beer suggested by some garden columnists entice my dog, but do not attract the slugs. However, slug baits containing meta do work. Slip it under rocks or matted plants to prevent easy access for birds, pets, or tiny children, since it is poisonous. Or place inverted jar lids lightly over the bait to keep it dry. The slugs will seek it out, and it will kill them.

Slugs are always worst during hot, wet summers. We have one species which is at least two inches long. It leaves a slimy trail on the ground that is a giveaway if you're wondering what's eating your plants. The small slugs can be just as bad. Go out with a flashlight to check after the sun goes down if you're suspicious. Sometimes you will find a whole plant full of them gnawing away.

The round slug eggs are laid in masses and look like tiny pearls. Often you will find them during spring or fall cleanup, especially under rocks and logs. Scoop them up and burn them.

Insects, mildews, and diseases do attack American plants, but on the whole I would say the natives suffer from fewer such disasters than highly bred garden stock. You still need to use good garden practices. One of the best is to diversify what you grow. Adding some of these American perennials to your existing garden is a step in the right direction. With a number of different genera growing together, a single insect or disease is less likely to lay the whole garden low. Encouraging a resident bird population is a great aid, too. Nesting pairs of birds eat unbelievable numbers of insects.

In years of high population growth, you may have to spray against particular insects such as Japanese beetles or inch worms, but your natives certainly will be no more affected than anything else. Should some plants become diseased, dispose of the foliage quickly to prevent the disease spreading.

Adequate water is most important to the health of your plants, but try to do your hosing in daylight hours so that the foliage of plants is dry before nightfall and cooling temperatures. This single practice greatly reduces the incidence of mildew and fungus. Few of your native perennials are gross feeders, but the tilth of your soil with high humus content is very important for good root development. Woodland plants are seldom improved by any fertilizing, and many would resent it. Some of the plants suggested for sunny gardens, however, do benefit from the same feeding you give other plants. Most of the sunny-section plants will not mind if you include them in feedings given their near neighbors.

By and large you will have much less trouble from pests and disease with your native plant material than with such highly susceptible plants as roses. This is especially true if you take trouble to site the plants correctly. Such intelligent placement makes for healthy plants all around. And it makes your job easier if you don't have to be continually catering to them because they're in the wrong kind of environment. That's why it is so important to match the plant to the site available.

Do You Have a Plan?

Included in this chapter are a number of garden plans. They are only suggestions of how to use American perennials. You can adapt them any way you please. Note the compass readings, however. If your garden faces in a different direction from that drawn in a plan, your plantings should be adjusted. This is because of the difference in available sunlight.

Some very lovely gardens just sort of grow. One of my own favorites started with one dogwood. Since that tree was the only living thing on the property aside from a few struggling blades of grass, the outcome was almost preordained. Eventually, it was joined by several other trees and some shrubs. Meanwhile I was planting bulbs and perennials beneath and around the trees. As the baby trees cast more shade, I had to revamp the garden and move sun-loving plants out from under the leaf canopy. Before that time arrived, I hadn't given too much thought to the garden as a whole. I'd been smart enough to plant some shade-loving species on the north side of the original tree, but the speed with which the developing trees cast more shadow caught me by surprise. I had not thought much about the mature size of the trees when I put them in.

This should give you an important hint about planning any garden area: it will never remain the same, and some idea of the eventual size and height of any tree should be taken into consideration before you plant it. To be truthful, I have never worked with a garden plan to exact scale on graph paper, although that technique is one of the best. My garden plans are scribbled on the backs of old envelopes or drawn so small I can hardly read them. But I am essentially an impatient, lazy, untidy person. If my plans were drawn closer to scale, I would not continually run out of space between two planned groupings of plants.

You should at least recognize that it is a lot easier to move a tree or a colony of plants on paper than in the ground. You can save yourself a lot of future grief and tired muscles if you outline your gardens on paper first. Most books on trees and shrubs will give you some dimensions for mature specimens. With a dogwood tree, for example, which has a horizontal spread of at least ten feet by the time it reaches its young teens, you should not plant it closer to another tree than at least that ten feet. Even at that the branches of the two will interlace.

Another factor when planning is to start out with the intention of creating gardens, not tiny beds here and there. You get much more effect for much less work if you site your trees so that they are parts of a whole rather than separate beds. There is less trimming of edges, and the whole looks better and bigger than when a lawn is broken up with little circles or thin strips.

The smaller your property the more imperative some sort of plan will be. You do not want to waste those few precious square feet but, rather, get from them the most garden possible. Paradoxically, lack of planning shows up much more strikingly in the small garden than in a larger tract.

When you are planning, keep the seasons in mind. Some color, if only from a tiny evergreen dwarf like paxistima or a small patch of red-berried wintergreen, brings delight all out of proportion to size during the dead winter months. Many woodland plants bloom in the spring, so try to add a few like Solomon-plume, which has good summer foliage, or hypoxis and wild bleeding-heart, which produce flowers until frost. The sunny summer border may need special attention to stretch its bloom for spring and fall.

If conditions are to their liking, many plants will eventually seed themselves. You can start out your planned patches with two or three plants initially if your budget is tight. The self-sown plants, which will be interspersed with each other in time, will give a desired natural look for the woodland garden. In a formal border, however, transplant seedlings to make large groupings of individual species or give away your excess. Even in a woodland, you will achieve maximum effect if you work toward large groupings of similar plants.

Too much variety creates an unpleasing hodgepodge, but you do want some contrast in height, size, flower color, and leaf shape. The bold spires of thermopsis, liatris, or burnet have one effect. Little creepers like wild ginger or tiarella have still another. Plants with an arching pattern such as the Solomon-seal or the fountainlike growth of polemonium and amsonia add interest for the eye.

When you draw up your plan, allow for shady and sunny areas

as dictated by the existing trees and bushes or by structures of any kind. The conditions available dictate what plants you can successfully grow. Remember that it will be sunny under deciduous trees until the leaves are full grown, and many woodland plants revel in just such circumstances.

Keep the growth habits and heights of the various plants in mind as you position them on your plan. Creepers and groundcovers or very low plants usually belong in the foreground. Taller plants go toward the back unless needed for an accent of some sort. Repeating a plant or a grouping in a garden is a very effective technique.

Try to think ahead. Does one plant go dormant soon after flowering? If so, its space will be blank during the rest of the season. Will this matter to your garden design? Perhaps you need to plant something else with it to take over later. Or will a fountainlike plant in front or behind the blank space adequately hide it?

If you find that your garden has too much blue or that its flowering is all concentrated in one season, start looking for species which will add other colors or bloom during other months of the growing year. Take into consideration also the decorating effects of interesting long-lived foliage, fall color, and possible berries or seedpods.

Remember that the plan is only a guide. Undoubtedly you will change some parts after you see the garden growing. Keep notes during the seasons to jog your memory. Sometimes I stick labels in the garden to remind me where I want a future planting to be situated.

Many times two plants complement each other to create a far stronger garden picture than either does by itself. I am very fond of polemonium with late tulips, for example. *Phlox divaricata* and wild bleeding-heart were made for each other, and white crested iris is breathtaking in front of red columbine. Whenever you notice two plants that have the same blooming season and the same habitat requirements, consider whether they would make a good pair.

Other gardens will give you ideas, and so will careful study of catalogs. Rather than treat these latter simply as lists of what is available, you should use them as textbooks. The descriptions of

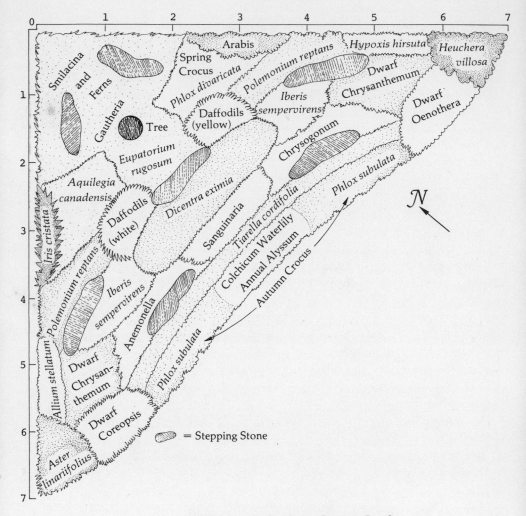

All-Season Color for a Corner Garden

If the boundaries of this garden consist of closed fencing or building walls, there will be less light for the plants. Substitute species that like more shade if necessary.

height, site preference, color, and bloom period are all details you need for planning a really great garden. And in the winter watches, when you must perforce spend most of your gardening time indoors, delve into some of the books listed in the Bibliography, which give more information on American native material. Gardening magazines and shows are other good sources of ideas. Research for a plant to fill a blank can be a most rewarding endeavor.

Which Way Is South?

Before you do any more planning or planting, make sure you know the points of the compass in reference to your property. This is an important factor to consider even when buying land and house. If your preference is for a sunny garden, you must have clear open land. There can be trees to the north, even somewhat to the east, but there must be open space for the sun to shine in at least from south and west. If the position of the house and trees on the property is such that there is no open space with a southern exposure, you might as well forget about growing roses and vegetables as well as a whole host of other plants that want nearly a full day of sunlight.

If on the other hand, your desire is for a woodland or shady garden, you must have room to site it where the trees cast their shade. A thin windbreak or strip of trees along your property line to the north will cast most of its shadow onto the next property. Perhaps by planting a few well-chosen trees in the right spot on your own property, you can extend the shaded portion so that you have some of your own.

How Does the Land Lie?

Gardens should be laid out to follow the topography of the land, too. If you have a hillside on your property, the best garden will follow the slope of the hill, not cut across it at some strange angle. Take advantage of every elevation or hollow. The low spot where water from main roof drains collects may be the nucleus of

Sunny Border with Emphasis on American Perennials

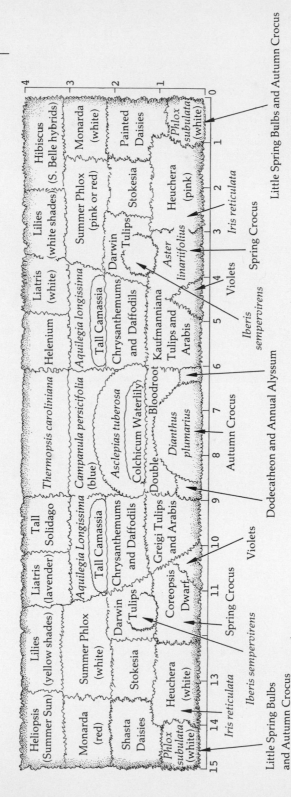

American perennials are the main denizens of this sunny garden. For a longer border, simply repeat the basic plantings. Some plants such as the monarda will spread beyond their boundaries unless you remove extra off-sets. The tallest plants are set in the back both for effect and to allow maximum sunshine for all the plants.

a semiwet garden. A tree or bush chosen for such a site because of its preference for wet feet will reward you handsomely. Around its periphery ferns and some of the moisture-loving plants will help change a problem spot into a pretty oasis. Conversely, a steep slope can be terraced and made into a most effective garden for bulbs and all the other plants that thrive on well-drained soil. Such treatment will be a lot easier than trying to get grass to grow on the hill or mowing it afterward.

If you have a brook, a garden following its course is almost impossible not to want. Paths, patios, driveways, play areas, possible viewing from the house, and proximity to the house as protection against marauding deer are additional factors that need to be considered when deciding where to put a garden. So is a location within reasonable reach of the hose. I once planted elderberries in a low spot at the very edge of our property. It was fine when it rained, but I could not drag that much hose around. Above all, make your garden something you want, not what the whole neighborhood seems to favor unless that is your desire, too.

All of which leads to one final thought: no plant whether tree, bush, or groundcover exists all by itself. Whenever I lecture or write about one particular facet of gardening, I like to close with a plea about the whole garden. No more than any other group of plants, our natives should not be grown as the end-all of a garden. I suppose you could grow some of the shade-lovers with the protection of a lath covering or an elaborate screen, but common sense tells us they grow best under the shelter of trees and bushes just as they do in the wild.

No matter what its size, a true garden is made up of many elements. Some are inorganic: birdbaths, paths, benches, buildings, walls, or large rocks. Others are differing types of growing things: groundcovers, ferns, trees, shrubs, bulbs. All have their place in the scheme of the perfect garden (or as close to it as any of us will ever get this side of Eden). This book was written to focus attention on what one gardener considers the best native perennials for cultivated gardens. It is by no means a conclusive list, nor is it meant to exclude from the garden a great host of valuable plants from all over the world. Use as many of them as you want and need.

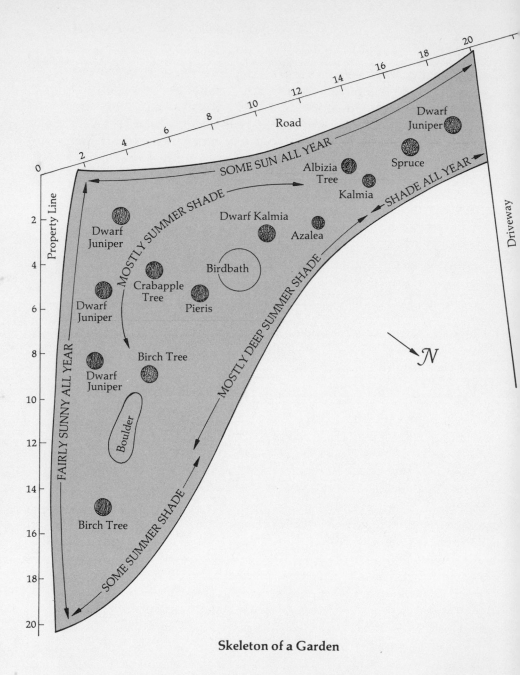

Skeleton of a Garden

Trees and shrubs were planted first in this garden to give the property more privacy from the road. Small plants to fill in are chosen according to available amount of light at various times of year. Such planning makes for less work and healthier plants. You will need to inspect the garden at different times of day and in all four seasons to get the best idea of the possibilities of light and shade.

One plant only begins a garden. In the larger sense no garden ever becomes complete. Tastes vary, conditions change, and gardeners become old coping with both mistakes and successes. Its very changeability is what makes gardening a fascinating activity. Please use this book as a starting place and try to create whole gardens, not tiny microcosms.

2
Plant Hardiness

Europeans are often bewildered by the wide range of climates encompassed by the United States and southern Canada. Even excluding Hawaii, Alaska and the vast expanses of arctic and subarctic Canada, just about every extreme of hot and cold or dry and wet exists in some corner of the great area between the Fiftieth parallel and the Rio Grande. The various plants native to that tremendous expanse have very different needs. In choosing the plants to include in this book, I have concentrated on those that have the widest ranges.

Obviously, they will not all grow everywhere. Living in the temperate climate of the mid-Atlantic states, I have tried to remember how important the hardiness of a plant can be to gardeners in areas where the winter temperatures are very low. We here in the Philadelphia area are likely to try almost anything, and quite often we succeed. Our climate is such that with a little help many southern species will get through our winters. Far northern plants need care because our summers are too hot. Oddly enough, it is these latter that are more likely to fail here. I have not included many real alpine plants in the recommended listings because making them at home outside their natural mountainous habitat can be quite tricky. Nor are there any far southern species which cannot take some frost.

Unfortunately, the hardiness limits of many of our native plants have not been determined. Until more gardeners admit them to cultivation, we will not know this important determinant. Your own experiments will add to the total knowledge. In the descriptions of the selected 100 individual species I have given the natural range of the plant as defined in Gray's *Manual of Botany*. Knowing that a plant may be found growing in both Ontario and Louisiana gives gardeners an idea of its wide-ranging adaptability. When I am certain that a plant is garden-hardy farther north than found in the wild, I have so reported. It is worth emphasizing that there may well be strains of the same plant with different ranges of hardiness. If you live at one end or the other of the hardiness scale, it becomes more important where you obtain your stock. In the Appendix is a long list of possible suppliers. Where you have a choice, try to obtain plants from a dealer whose climate is closest to your own. You cannot have much control over where seed comes from, but plants are more likely to have been raised or collected near the dealer's headquarters.

Again, common sense is a good suggestion. With winters that register zero once in a while, I certainly do not expect subtropical species to survive here outdoors. Plants that are only semihardy need help here most winters either by protective mulching or initial placement. Every gardener likes challenges, but obviously the bulk of growing material in any one garden should be species that will survive the local extreme of either hot or cold without great trouble on your part.

Our worst problem here is winter heaving. We do not have snow cover for long periods during the winter, and our temperatures tend to jump up and down. Our soil does not freeze deeply; and its upper crust, in areas where the sun reaches it, is subjected to alternate periods of freeze and thaw. This is death for many seedling plants, particularly those that have tuberous or tap roots rather than a mass of fibrous roots. A midwinter garden tour can disclose roots forced completely out of the ground. Unless gently covered or pushed back quickly, these roots will dry out and die. Once they have a few seasons to put out small side roots as anchors, however, such tuberous plants as butterflyweed are quite safe.

To solve this problem I do two things. First, I start these perennials from seed very early in the spring so that they can develop as good a root system as possible before their first winter. Second, they are often wintered over that first crucial year in a fairly protected spot with a good mulch of leaves and bark added by Christmas, when the frost usually is in the ground. Shade or a position facing north are best for such a nursery site, since such a spot freezes up and stays that way. Of course, such plantings are inspected during the winter, and the roots pushed back if necessary. When I can, I also transplant such seedlings to their permanent homes early in their second spring so they can put down a secure root system for a long life before there is any hint of the next winter. The farther north you live, the chancier becomes late-summer transplanting.

Herbaceous plants on which the tops die down in winter are easier to cultivate north of their natural limits than those which are evergreen. Good drainage helps, and so does the proper kind of loose, friable soil, which encourages good root development. Where there is reliable snow cover, it acts as a protective blanket. This helps many gardeners who live farther north than I. A light organic mulch substitutes for snow, but never as adequately. Wind protection and a spot not touched by the first morning rays of the sun are always helpful for those plants that bloom or start growth very early in spring.

Some mention should be made of micro-climates. There are always spots on even the smallest property where the lay of the land and the placement of buildings tempers the climate. To the south of a building, wall, large boulder, or evergreen it is always a bit warmer. The snow melts first there, and the frost never goes as deep. There the first flowers of spring and the last of fall can be encouraged, but only after such plants have developed good root systems; after all, such a spot is more apt to experience heaving in the upper inch or so than one where the frost goes in and stays all winter.

My present house creates another interesting micro-climate. About two feet along the front of the house, which faces southwest, is a spot that almost never freezes. This is partly because of position toward the sun, but it is also because there is a slight overhang of the roof at that point so that rain seldom enters the soil. During other seasons I can water plants there, but in winter anything in that area is nearly completely dry. It has proven a successful site for several plants that dislike wet and cold.

Another place to locate is the lee side of your house or of any outbuildings or large evergreen plantings. This is the spot least affected by the prevailing winter wind of your area. For us this is on the southeast side. The amount of shade, the type of soil, and the drainage are also limiting factors for what plants will grow where, but winter wind can be a dreadful killer. Such lee sites are my favorite for semihardy evergreen plants. The combination of winter sun and high drying wind can actually burn the foliage of such plants to the point where it dies. Sun reflected from a white house does funny things, too, and sometimes burns plants in winter, but this is more important for shrubs than smaller ground-hugging plants.

Remember as well that cold air is heavier than warm air and moves downhill. When gardeners shudder about "frost pockets," they are talking about such low spots. It actually is colder at the foot of a hill than at the top. Gardeners in such low areas where the cold air is trapped by the topography will find their plants blacken with frost even weeks earlier than their luckier neighbors. Low-lying gardens wake up later in the spring as well, and the soil may not be warm enough or dry enough to work as early either.

However, poor drainage and cold are not always a drawback. Cardinal flowers often do better where frozen water in the soil acts as a sort of protective factor. You may want to locate a frost pocket because you are trying to carry far northern plants through too-hot weather. These cooler spots are the wiser choice for such genera. Shade, of course, is the greatest aid, and adequate water in hot periods the second factor for such horticultural finagling. As a rule of thumb, the farther south of its natural haunts a plant is being grown, the greater its need for some shade. This is true even for plants that are normally found in full sun in the north. Locate these aliens so that they have afternoon protection from the summer sun to give them the best chance of survival. A cooling period of misty hosing also brings down the temperature around a plant on a torrid day.

Altitude makes a difference in climate just as much as distance north or south. You will note that some plants have natural ranges which follow the mountains south into Georgia, Alabama, and Tennessee. These are northern species that find suitable habitats in the coolness of the higher altitudes in those states. They are not found in hot coastal areas.

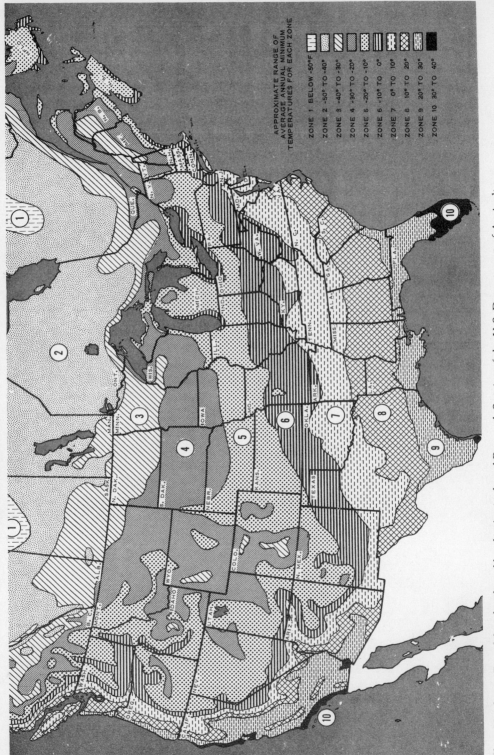

ZONE 1 BELOW -50°F
ZONE 2 -50° TO -40°
ZONE 3 -40° TO -30°
ZONE 4 -30° TO -20°
ZONE 5 -20° TO -10°
ZONE 6 -10° TO 0°
ZONE 7 0° TO 10°
ZONE 8 10° TO 20°
ZONE 9 20° TO 30°
ZONE 10 30° TO 40°

APPROXIMATE RANGE OF
AVERAGE ANNUAL MINIMUM
TEMPERATURES FOR EACH ZONE

Plant Hardiness Zone Map developed by the Agricultural Research Service of the U.S. Department of Agriculture.

Having a large lake or river nearby again influences your climate, and the oceans have an even greater impact, especially if a large current such as the Gulf Stream is involved. You will note on the hardiness-zone map that the kinder zones go farther north nearer the oceans and the Great Lakes just as the colder zones reach long fingers into the south along the mountain ranges. The bodies of water make it cooler in summer and warmer in winter. On a much smaller scale, even a pond or a small brook will provide somewhat mitigating circumstances. If you do not already know it, locate your garden on the zone-hardiness map as best you can. It will give you some insight into what you can do. It's always a bit unnerving to the neophyte gardener to realize that the winter on Cape Cod is similar to that found in the mountains of Alabama, or that the climate of the mountain areas of California resembles that of West Virginia.

All these points are ways to stretch your garden's potential. They make it possible to grow some surprises, to assimilate some beautiful aliens into your lifestyle. All of which is fun, but if you spent all your gardening in such pursuits, you'd soon grow tired of the trying. To repeat: most of the inhabitants of any garden ought to be plants that are at home there. Given the correct siting and a chance for their particular needs for sun, soil, and water, they should prosper without a great deal of trouble on your part. A garden, after all, ought to be a place to enjoy.

If you are new to this wonderful world of growing things, you will be wondering where to start. One of the best ways is to look at gardens nearby. Neighbors, parks, botanical gardens—all give you some idea of what does well where you live.

The 100 perennial natives listed in the plant section have been selected for their garden worthiness. Not every garden can contain all of them. They cover a wide spectrum of habitats and uses. The preceding chapter on garden sites is of at least as much importance to the health of your plants as is the problem of hardiness. And proper siting also makes your gardening easier as well as far more beautiful in results.

3
Obtaining Plants

Having studied your property and climate as objectively as possible, you will have a fairly good idea of what kinds of American plants you will be concentrating on. At least in the beginning direct your efforts for the easiest general site: mostly sunny, mostly shaded, or mostly wet. There is nothing like some successful experience to whet your interest in further gardening. It is much more rewarding to have a small, well-grown garden than a group of half-finished projects.

If your first preference is for plants that want sunshine, locating a commercial source is just a bit easier. Seed and/or plants of some of the most popular Americans for sun are offered by many of the general seedsmen and nurseries. They will also carry a few of the shade-lovers, but better, more complete lists of woodland plants are available from dealers who specialize in native material. I don't know why this is. A shady garden is often more likely to take care of itself than a sunny border, but the big houses have concentrated on the sun-loving plants. A good percentage of the moisture-loving plants will also be found through dealers in native plants, but those that live directly in the water, such as waterlilies and lotus, are more apt to be carried by aquatic specialists. I have listed a few of these latter in the Appendix; addresses for others may be obtained through the advertisements in any good garden magazine.

To Buy or Collect?

The one thing I want to avoid in this book is suggesting that you decorate your garden with trophies of rape and pillage from the nearest woodland, park, or roadside. That is one reason I have gone to considerable trouble to assemble a comprehensive list of suppliers. Almost always, buying a plant is preferable to obtaining one from the wild. At least in the highly populated northeast, the remaining wild stands need all the help they can get.

There are those who would defend collecting plants in the wild by some statement such as, "We left some plants to go to seed." Nonsense. There are only a finite number of plants in wild stands. Some of the loveliest natives were never plentiful. Even if everyone took only one plant, the wild plantations cannot possibly keep up with the demand any more. This may sound incredible to a collector standing knee-deep in flowers in a remote clearing of the Appalachians. But those of us who live closer to civilization's progress know only too well that there are annually fewer and fewer locations where really choice wildflowers proliferate. Acquiring a small amount of ripe seed from a natural stand is the only defensible act today in the northeast except where the bulldozer is actively at work. I am told that certain lilies native to the far western mountains are already rare because of indiscriminate collecting, so I take a very firm stand here for the entire country.

What compounds the sin of collecting from the wild is that most of the plants so acquired will die. In nature there is seldom a soft bed of earth ready for a seed. Each must take its chances, and often the resulting seedling must send long roots around rocks or other barriers to find the nourishment and moisture necessary for the plant's well-being. Instead of a compact, fibrous mass of roots such as is found in nursery-grown stock, the wild plant subsists with a few widely wandering roots. The collector cannot possibly dig them up adequately. Moreover, to locate the plant at all in a wild spot, the collector usually arrives while the plant is in active growth, rather than during its dormant period. To transplant successfully under these conditions, you must pot and nurse the plants carefully. Even experts often fail at such an attempt.

The one exception to all of this is when "progress" is headed for a section of land particularly rich in native plants. Then the best course of action is to organize a real expedition of interested people with at least one expert present to indicate what is most important to save. Get permission from the owners, of course, and try to time the effort for early spring or late summer, when the plants are most likely to have the best chance of surviving the action. Take along ice chests if it is warm and a large supply of water even if it's not. And don't forget some kind of labeling system. Individual plants or sods of groundcovers can be dug with as much root and original soil as practical, placed in plastic bags, watered well, and kept shaded at all times. Transplanting must not be delayed. If you organize your group well, you will have some site to which plants will be brought for careful nursing through a season. Sometimes you can interest a plant sanctuary or a botanical garden in sponsoring such an effort. On a small scale you can do such a job yourself; but if the spot is really worthwhile, you accomplish more with adequate aid.

How, you ask, am I to get plants if I cannot collect? To which I answer; just the way you get any other kind of plants for your garden. Either raise them yourself from seed or buy from a dealer. Some of the latter still collect, and for obvious reasons I prefer to use those who raise their own. When you see an ad for "collected plants," at least realize this is not prime stock for transplanting.

One at least hopes the dealer recognizes what's at stake and does some propagating of his own. The nice thing about plants acquired by some form of artificial propagating is that they are easier to move. Raised in beds of prepared soil, they produce compact root systems, which take transplanting much better. Thus morally and financially, you are ahead of the game.

Much mail-order stock must of necessity be sent nearly bare-root because of cost. Except in earliest spring, such plants are best potted in a soil mixture containing plenty of peat moss immediately after receipt. Keep them shaded and well watered for a few weeks until new leaf growth assures you they have started new root growth. They can then be knocked out carefully from the pots and planted in the garden with a minimum of loss. There is more about transplanting in the next chapter.

Try to get your orders in as early as possible so that your plants arrive at prime times. For early spring-flowering species, late summer may be a time of dormancy, and plants can take transplanting best then. Many dealers have stock available for fall planting. For the less experienced gardener, however, spring planting may be a better choice because it gives the plants a whole season in which to acclimatize themselves and get a good root system before winter. This is particularly important where frost goes into the ground early.

Given a choice, buy from a dealer whose climate is similar to your own. His plants may be a trifle hardier under your conditions, although that is not a hard-and-fast rule. What is more important, they will be more apt to arrive at the right time for transplanting in your latitude. I have sometimes had an order from a southern dealer appear on my porch while my garden was still frozen and unworkable or one from the north not arrive until it was already torrid here. Nearby garden centers are also possible places to locate stock, and some of them also specialize in native plants. The nearest horticultural society, garden club, botanical garden, or nature preserve will be able to give you suggestions on where to obtain plants locally.

It is hoped that as more and more gardeners realize that native plants represent fine garden decoratives, it will be easier to obtain what you want. For now, the mail-order houses listed in the Appendix are to be highly commended for the job they have been doing. Those that are willing to take the trouble to propagate superior forms of our American plants are the real stars.

Please note that many dealers exact a charge for their catalogs. Since many wildflower specialists are fairly small outfits, they simply cannot shoulder the complete costs of printing and mailing. Unfortunately some dealers are getting on in years, and some of the best dealers in native plants have gone out of business in the past decade. All those listed were still going as of the beginning of 1976. Some of the more expensive catalogs are good for several seasons.

Sports, Hybrids, and Selections

The serious gardener can only applaud the increasing number of hybrids and selections of American plants that are now on the market. Nature itself has been hybridizing and selecting since time began, and man's achievements are no less to be enjoyed.

The hybrid plant tends to have more vigor, more adaptability, and often larger flowers in a greater range of colors. The crossing of two different parent species doubles the possible chromosome combinations in a more sophisticated way than just using two different plants of the same species for cross pollination. Improvements in habit, foliage, or healthiness as well as size are often the result. Such a process takes time and patience. But a comparison of the modern summer phlox hybrids with their wild ancestors will be enough to convince any gardener that it is well worth the effort involved. The greatest advances readily apparent are in the flowers themselves. Take a look at a modern nursery catalog. The wide range of phlox in a bewildering number of colors is proof enough that our gardens are the richer for such work. Botanically such hybrids are called cultivars, and they have names, often quite fancifully descriptive, given by the originator. These are capitalized in Roman type in the catalogs: *Phlox* Miss Lingard or *P.* Starfire, for example.

Selections are superior species forms found either in the wild or in batches of plants from seed. Even the most amateur gardener might come across one, particularly if raising plants this way in any quantity. Again, those in the trade are most likely to be variations in flower color or size, but sometimes other favorable characteristics are apparent enough for selection to be made by some observant gardener. I have one planting of *Chrysogonum virginianum*, for example, which year after year blooms longer than the others. A smart nurseryman might propagate it as an "everblooming" selection. Some selections are actually varieties, that is, a group of plants known to occur in the wild and differing slightly from others of the same species but not enough to become another species. They may be written as *Phlox divaricata* var. *laphami* or *Phlox stolonifera* Blue Ridge. One is a botanical variety, the other a commercial selection. The former may or may not be a better garden form, but the latter almost always is.

Some selections or varieties are "sports." These are mutations that occur in nature for unexplained reasons. Those in commerce usually deviate from the norm rather widely. One famous native sport is the gorgeous double form of bloodroot, *Sanguinaria canadensis* var. *flora plena.* Some mutations are no improvement to a genus; a double-headed flower is no prettier than a two-headed calf. But those in which the inherited characteristic doubles the petals or results in some other desirable trait represent a gift from nature. The sharp-eyed gardener is always on the lookout for these plants, and a few have made a tidy sum by propagating and selling such discoveries.

It is not always easy to tell in catalog listings whether a named cultivar is a hybrid or a selection or a sport. With few exceptions, however, such named plants are an improvement over the species and worth trying.

The hybrid cultivar, the selection, and some sports must all be vegetatively reproduced. Their progeny from seed may not show any deviation from the norm or, in the case of hybrids, may represent a throwback to one of the parents. So these more desirable forms are propagated by cuttings, division, or other means. Each new plant is really a piece of the original, which first showed the desirable trait. It is understandable that such forms may be more expensive than those for which plants can be easily obtained by the hundreds merely by sowing seeds. In practice, however, raising from cuttings or division can be a shortcut to mature plants. Do check directions for these procedures in the propagating chapter. With many plants it is much faster and easier to propagate vegetatively. If you need many plants of a given species or variety, you will certainly find it much cheaper in the long run to buy a start of some desired plant and learn to increase it yourself.

We must give a fervent thank you to the dealers who are willing to take the time and money to perpetuate good forms or hybrids. You can be sure that such businesses are not raping wild stands, too. Many of the hybrids and even some of the selections are of European origin. Our native plants represented something new in that part of the world. Europeans could see garden possibilities in plants which too many Americans dismissed as weeds. Take, for example, the European introductions of hybrid goldenrod, asters, and phlox—all of them accomplished with stock that originally came from this side of the ocean. It is to be hoped that our coming of age botanically will inspire American botanists and plantsmen to do more hybridizing and selecting with the native species. I personally think we have gone about as far as necessary with such introduced plants as hybrid petunias and marigolds. One new hybrid of these hardly differs from another.

Here and there American horticulturalists have been doing some interesting work in this sphere, so perhaps the tide is changing. Not long ago I was quite electrified to see the results of crossing the red *Lobelia cardinalis* with the blue *L. siphilitica.* Kingwood Center in Mansfield, Ohio, has some very interesting results of this particular cross. And there are American dealers propagating some of the selections and some of the rare white forms. The two lobelias just mentioned both have such albinos, and they have entered into the hybridizing programs.

As we appreciate more just what a wonderful natural legacy we North Americans have, there will be more demand for improved forms. This will stimulate dealers to greater efforts, and gardens all over the world will benefit. Despite those hopes for the future, I can categorically promise you that there already exists a vast treasure of American perennials that offer you easy and beautiful garden decoration. Many of the species are quite perfect just the way they are, but I would not be so foolish as to discourage hybridizing of any sort. I happen to adore the eastern wild bleeding-heart, for example, but there are now some hybrids between it and the western species that have great garden merit.

4
Propagating
and Transplanting

As any biologist will tell you, plants could get along quite nicely on earth without man, or any other animal, for that matter. Even if you do nothing at all, your plants will propagate themselves to some extent from seed, creeping roots, or offsets. Some of these processes you may even want to slow down or discourage. You will note that in many of the species descriptions to follow you are advised to remove old flower heads before seed forms. This technique fosters longer flowering in many genera, and it keeps hybrid strains true, since the seedlings of such plants are seldom on a par with the hybrid parent. In some cases deheading, as it is often termed, cuts down on future weeding because some plants self-sow to an overwhelming extent if left to their own devices.

Just as often you will want to produce in some quantity more plants of a particular species or even of a selection or hybrid. To be able to do so certainly cuts down on the expense of developing a larger garden. The smart gardener buys a start of a desired plant, then raises more until the desired number has been reached. Moreover, some types of plants are just not available in quantity. Or perhaps your only source of supply is a packet of seeds. What with one thing and another, almost every gardener does some propagating of some sort. We have room for only a brief summary of the most important ways, but I would warn you this is a fascinating part of horticulture.

From Seed

Starting plants from seed is probably the easiest method of propagation. Nearly every species here described can be reproduced this way, although some more easily than others. In some cases in the species descriptions you will find directions to sow seed as soon as ripe in summer or fall, this because the seed has proved to have a very short viable period (during which it will germinate) or because it requires a very long stretch of changing temperatures to break inherent dormancy.

However, seed of most of the plants we are dealing with does not have to be sown in the fall. But you cannot wait until the kinder days of spring either, as you do with marigolds, which are not sown until the soil has warmed up. Our 100 American plants are all perennials, most of them from areas where there is some winter weather. The best and easiest technique is to sow this seed somewhere between January and early March. Flats filled with an equal mixture of loam, peat, and coarse sand can be prepared before winter sets in and left in the garage until time for use. They need not be formal wooden flats either. Large pots or milk cartons with one side cut out and drainage holes punched in the bottom work just as well. The essential point is that the seed be sown early, and the flats be put outside. In most climates they will not need additional watering after the initial one following sowing unless they are placed in a covered area. It is much better to put them right out in the weather. Choose a spot that faces toward the north but has good light. Like all seeds, these should be covered with a thin layer of soil after sowing. Very fine seed is best just sprinkled on the soil surface and then gently pressed in. If rodents and birds are a problem, protect the flats with a piece of screening.

Admittedly, you could sow the seed in the fall when the soil is prepared, but it usually works just as well to do it later; then the flats are subjected to a shorter period of time in which something unfavorable might happen to their contents. The problem is that most of these seeds require a period of cold first and then germinate when the soil gets to around 40°F. If there are some that germinate at lower or higher temperatures, the fluctuating outside temperatures will give them the opportunity. What you need to remember is that many of the most popular garden annuals, like marigolds, are plants native to warmer climates than ours; in their original homes they may even be perennial. But they cannot take cold, and so we sow their seed after our soils and nights have warmed up. Our own natives evolved to meet a climate that has a cold winter. Their seed has a built-in factor that usually retards their sprouting in the warm fall days. They must have the cold first to break the inherent dormancy of the seed so it can germinate.

Once in a while nothing happens to a flat of seed. The seed may have been too old; insects may have eaten it. Lots of hazards exist, but sometimes a plant is a really late bloomer, if I may be allowed a bad pun. It may actually germinate the second spring, so it is worthwhile to save the flat in an out-of-the-way spot and let it go through a second winter before discarding. Bulbous plants are especially prone to this delayed germination.

What are you to do if you cannot procure the seed early enough to do this winter planting? Why, use your refrigerator of course. You could wait a season and plant them the next winter, but you will have lost a whole growing year that way, and some seeds lose their viability if they wait too long. If you are so late in getting your seed that the outside temperatures are already over 40°F. at night, open the packets—but do not remove the seed—and place them in a glass jar with a not-too-tight-fitting top. Note the date and leave them from four to eight weeks in the refrigerator before sowing. You will have to give them more attention after sowing because the weather will have grown quite warm by then; the seed flat must not dry out once planted.

This treatment of seeds needing a cold period before germinating is called stratification. Some gardeners prefer to put some damp sand into a glass jar or plastic bag and then shake the seed up in it and stratify it that way. The seed and sand mixture is then sown in a flat atop the soil after the period of stratification.

You can see why prompt early ordering is much the best policy for perennial seed of this sort. Most catalogs arrive right after Christmas, and the early list will arrive in time to do your outdoor planting for stratification. You can gauge which method to use by the last spring frost date for your area. If it does not occur until the end of April, you have at least until March before you need be concerned your flats will be too warm. Most seed does not require a long period of cold.

If you are dealing with a rare plant or one for which seed is difficult to find, don't put all your seed in one container. Hold some back. If your early spring planting does not succeed, sow another batch in late October or November and leave it outside all winter. It may turn out you are dealing with a seed that needs the longer period of stratification.

When you want just a modest increase of a plant you already have in the garden, the easiest technique of all is to sow some seed in the open ground near the parent plant as soon as it is ripe. Everything else being equal, such a procedure should result in a nice colony of seedlings with the least trouble. It is much wiser than just hoping the plant will self-sow, although that can happen, too.

Once the seedlings begin to appear in the flats, treat them just as with any other type of plant. Move them to a spot where there is good light, and for plants that are sun-lovers this will mean out into the open. Keep the soil moist so the tiny plants do not dry out. Plants that naturally grow in wet places require you to keep them wetter from start to final permanent planting.

Keep in mind that these are perennials you are raising. With a very few exceptions, they will not bloom their first year from seed. They need a full season to develop good root systems first, but then they will give you many years of pleasure. So the work you do that first year is really a worthwhile investment in the future of your garden. The prices of nursery-grown perennial plants you buy from a dealer reflect his efforts in the same vein.

Transplanting of the seedlings will be necessary once they have several pairs of true leaves. (The first pair are cotelydon or feeder leaves and often of a different shape from the true leaves.)

There are two courses of action open when you transplant the seedlings. One is to plant each in a separate pot. These containers are then buried up to their tops in nursery rows or kept close together in a flat. They are watered and fed as needed until fall or the next spring when they are easily knocked out of the pots and put into place where wanted in the garden. Winter heaving that first year is a problem with either action; a protective mulch helps combat this.

An alternative is to plant the seedlings immediately into the open garden where they can grow all their first summer. If you are only raising a few plants this way, this is often easier than potting, but it has several drawbacks. One is that during their earliest months the seedlings may not be able to compete with the full-sized plants in the garden. Another is that in periods of extreme drought or flooding rains, it is much easier to cater to small plants that are all in one place than to remember where several plantations of babies have been put in the garden.

If you do not want to pot, you will usually get thriftier, healthier mature plants if you transplant all the seedlings into a protected spot where the soil has good drainage and where you can keep a careful eye on them. You should separate the seedlings according to the amount of sun and shade they need. Baby plants want the same conditions as their full-grown counterparts. You may need one nursery bed for the sun-lovers and another in shade for the woodlanders. These plants are then best moved to their permanent homes early in their second spring. Some bloom usually occurs that year, and the plants then settle themselves in to make good clumps for many years of decoration.

If your need is for only a few specimens of a particular species, it may well be easier simply to buy them as plants. But if you want many, try to raise them from seed if only for the sake of your pocketbook.

There is another bonus to raising natives in quantity from seed: you may well discover one or more superior plants. The genes present in a strain of plants may have characteristics that do not show in the parents. With a large crop of seedlings, you are much more apt to find one or more with better foliage, bigger flowers, or even flowers with a more desirable color than the type. It is an interesting kind of challenge. As we have mentioned, the possibilities of selection for superior qualities have been only lightly touched so far for the vast number of American natives. Only heaven knows what wonder you might uncover.

If for some reason you have a need to gather seed in any quantity from your own stand of native plants, there is one way to ensure a better crop of seed. Always plant at least two or three individual plants; but if you can obtain one plant from a different source, your seed production may be even better. It is probable that if you obtain all your plants of a particular species from the same source, they will have many common traits. Cross pollination by bringing in a new line can add new chromosomal characteristics. You are not raising hybrids by this process, but you are loading the odds in your favor that you will have wider variety among the seedlings. You will certainly tend to get more fertile seeds from a given number of plants if they do not all have a common origin.

How to store seed from your own garden or leftovers from an order is another question. Above all, seed should be put in a cool spot where it cannot get wet. Labeled envelopes work as well as anything. It is not necessary to store in the refrigerator except as a shortcut for the cold period of stratification, but never store seed near a heat source.

Gathering seed is not difficult, but here are a few pointers. Most plants produce their seed in some kind of capsule. Those that don't are extremely hard to gather, incidentally; they will scatter the ripe seed with the slightest movement, and you will have to depend on self-sown plants if you are too late. When you are trying to gather a specific seed, remind yourself to check the plants in question continually after flowering is over. For the health of the mother plants it is a good idea to cut off some of the old flowers before seed forms; it does sometimes rob the parent plant to produce a big crop of mature seeds, so by halving the amount you ask it to develop you drain it less.

Ordinarily the seed capsule, which may take many odd forms, begins to lose its green color as the seed ripens. The time between when the pod is plump and green and when the seed is suddenly ripe can be very short. Eastern wild columbine, for example, will have nice ripe, shiny black seeds in capsules that still show green tints. Until you learn the idiocyncrasies of each plant, just keep peeking. Once the capsule is open, the seed is usually ripe. For good quantity, however, you should gather your crop just as the capsules are opening or even before. Generally, ripe seed is plump rather than wrinkled, hard rather than soft, black or brown rather than white or green.

Clean seed is easier to store than a supply full of pieces of the capsules. It is also better to plant. For one thing, you can better judge how many seeds you are shaking into a row if the envelope contains only seed instead of lots of chaff as well. For another, there seems to be less chance of fungi and diseases if you sow just seed instead of a seed-and-chaff mixture.

Some seed is easy to clean on the spot. Members of the pea family, for instance, are in pods that open easily, and the seeds can be rubbed out into a container in much the way you shuck green peas for the table. The columbine capsules open at the top, and I shake these without picking them directly into a small box right in the garden; picking them individually tends to let the other capsules on a stem leak out their seed at the same time. But-terflyweed pods are like any other milkweed. These I watch carefully as they develop. They are picked just as they begin to split but before the milkweed silk is dry. You can get very good at rubbing the ripe seed off the center of the seed capsule without disturbing the silk. The air around me in the garden on days when I do this often fills with a cloud of tiny parachutes as the discarded silks expand and take off into the wind—but minus those precious seeds. Often you will find you must make several visits on suc-ceeding days to gather seed from various plants as they ripen.

Very fine seed, such as that of the lobelias, is more difficult. Picking the capsules individually means losing much of the seed as you disturb the stalks. These are better cut carefully, stem and all, and placed in a large seamless bag where you can shake the seed out under controlled conditions.

If you have a lot of chaff mixed with the seed, you can separate it fairly well by shaking the seed into one half of a large cardboard boxtop held at a slight tilt and blowing the chaff away. The heavier seed will tend to roll toward the bottom of the box as you shake and blow.

Transplanting

Before we go into other means of propagation, a few more words about transplanting. Many gardeners have wonderful re-sults with their seed sowing and other types of reproduction, then lose most of the crop when it is transplanted. One of the reasons for my preferring to put my seedlings into pots at the first transplanting is that they may then be carefully knocked out later and planted in their permanent spots with very little disturbance.

One good watering, and they may not even realize they have been moved except to find more room for their roots.

When transplanting, always remember that such an action breaks off many of the tiny feeder roots, which the plants need to absorb moisture. Try to work as gently as possible. Choose a cool and cloudy day if possible. At least do the job in the shade if dealing with tiny seedlings.

If the soil in the garden is not soft and friable, dig a good-sized hole even for a small seedling and mix peat moss into the soil to make it easy for the transplant to put out new root hairs. Above all, be faithful about watering for some days afterward. If the weather trips you up and suddenly becomes torrid, mist the transplants if they begin to wilt. Just turn your hose to the finest misty spray and prop it so that it covers the spot in question during the hottest hours of the day. These precautions are worthwhile when doing any transplanting but of course most necessary when it is warmer. Smart gardeners get as much as possible of their transplanting done in earliest spring.

Few of our American natives are gross feeders. Put into the correct site habitat, they do not require frequent applications of fertilizer; indeed, most do better without such treatment. However, in the crucial days after seedlings are transplanted, you can often encourage good growth by a liquid feeding. Use any all-purpose fertilizer that is soluble in water, but mix it at only one quarter the recommended strength. House-plant fertilizers are easy to find and store, and work very well. For acid-loving plants there are special soluble fertilizers, and these are the better choice for many natives. Give the seedlings this treatment several times during their first month after the initial transplanting.

Even for sun-loving plants a bit of shade immediately after transplanting is helpful in hot weather. One easy way is to spread old needled evergreen branches atop the bed temporarily. During early spring transplanting such precautions may not be as necessary. In much of the country, late summer can produce some sizzling days, and gardeners have to be more careful when doing transplanting then.

Discard any old myths about doing your watering during the cool of the early morning or early evening. The plants need the extra moisture during the hottest part of the day, and you will do only good by giving it to them then. This rule, incidentally, holds for most plants in the garden. Artificial watering is much better done so that the foliage dries before nightfall. Not only does this give the plants protection against wilting when they need it most, but it also prevents buildup of mold and mildew, which come when plants go into the cooler nighttime hours in a wet condition.

You should be aware that misting against wilt in the heat is different from deep watering in times of drought. When you must do the latter, you want a soft spray of water over a long time so that it penetrates deeply into the soil. This gives mature plants a deep drink. It also tends to discourage their developing shallow roots. A good surface mulch helps to conserve soil moisture, by the way.

The plain dirt gardener always has to think about how deep a plant should go. Here again let common sense be your guide. If you can see a dirt mark on the stem of a plant, it is a good indication of at what depth it had been growing. Most herbaceous material is planted so the crowns where the new growth arises are just under the soil surface. Where winter is very severe, slightly deeper planting may be wise.

Make a hole large enough so the root mass can be laid out around it rather than jammed into a small excavation. Add some peat moss as you replace the earth around the roots and firm well. For plants put in during warm weather it is always a good idea to leave a slight saucerlike depression around the plants at the soil surface so you can water well. Usually that slight depression will fill in by itself over a season. Make the saucer in the soil before you add the covering top mulch.

Suppose you have an underground stem or bulb. For most of the plants treated in these pages it should go so there is about an inch or two of soil atop it. In heavy clay soils plant more shallowly than in sandy or humusy soils. Always prepare a bigger hole than the plant or root actually needs and always soften the earth at the bottom of the planting hole. This way a plant or root that wants greater depth has a chance. Many plants and bulbs are quite capable of pulling themselves farther down into the soil by the action of their roots. But they cannot do this unless the soil underneath is soft and friable. If you plant them too deeply to start with, they are quite likely to rot or simply give up. It would be safer to err on the shallow side, particularly if your soil is loamy and if you are adding a top mulch, as you should with new plants. With most herbaceous plants there are roots showing to indicate which end is down, and with most tubers and bulbs there is some kind of eye or shoot to show which end is up.

Vegetative Propagation

We mentioned earlier that hybrids and selections do not usually breed true from seed. To increase your stock of such plants you must use one of the methods of vegetative propagation. No sex or crossing of strains is involved. You simply take a piece of a particular plant and from it reproduce an exact copy, identical in every way with the original. Such new plants are termed "clones" in botany. They are actually a part of the mother plant which has been induced to root in some way to form another plant. With species that are easily rooted, fine mature specimens are possible in a shorter length of time through these means than by raising from seed.

LAYERING

Of the various vegetative processes used in propagating plants, this is one of the easiest. It works best for plants that have a matlike or creeping way of growing, but it can be tried with any plant that has stems supple enough to bend down to soil level without breaking. In its simplest version you merely put a clump of dirt (anchor it with a small rock if necessary) atop one of the stems of the plant, making sure that a growing tip is out in the air. In a season, roots may form at the part of the stem under the clod of dirt; new upright growth at that point will indicate success. (See figure 1.)

When the new growth is apparent, sever the stem that connects the new plant to the mother. Most gardeners leave the little new plant in place another full season to enable it to put out a good independent root system of its own before they move it. Plants such as partridgeberry or woodland phlox, which root readily this

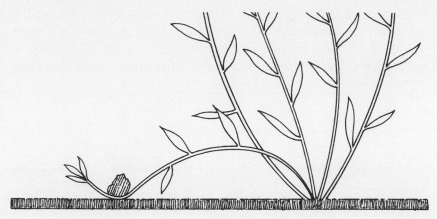

Figure 1

way, will even make layerings by themselves wherever a stem node touches the soil. With other plants, success may be better if the stem is first scratched with a fingernail or gently with a knife and the bruised portion treated with a root hormone powder before being pushed into the soil and covered with the clump of dirt. You can, if you wish, dig a shallow hole in which to press the stem to be layered, but don't put too much strain on the stem by overbending lest it break.

DIVISION

Just as easy is dividing large plants that obviously have many shoots arising independently in a clump rather than from a single main stem. Some vigorous growers like hybrid phlox or asters increase so well by themselves this way that there is a real danger they will smother themselves after a few seasons of growing. You can keep them healthier if you divide them. Unneeded extra plants so produced are nice gifts for a neighbor or a donation to a plant sale.

The simplest way is to lift the whole clump gently from the earth. If it is very large, use two spades or cultivating forks, one on either side to pry the clump out. Then pry apart or chop the big plants into smaller ones either with a spade or with a small hatchet. (See figure 2.) New growth is better for replanting than the

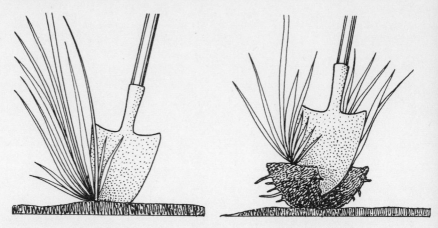

Figure 2

woodier, older center. Make sure some roots are left with each piece, replant where wanted, water well, and you are done. Early spring is the optimum time to do this; but with plants that bloom early, it can also be done later in the season. If you plan this operation for a plant that goes dormant after flowering, make sure you mark the site well so you can find it without serious injury to the roots. Spring division is recommended because then plants have a whole growing season in which to recover, but to do it then with a plant that blossoms early may be to sacrifice all bloom for that one year. A rule of thumb: divide summer- and fall-flowering plants in spring and spring-flowering plants in late summer.

Plants such as bloodroot or Solomon-seal, which produce underground stems or rhizomes, can be divided, too, and it is usually done while the tops are dormant. Dig up the branching roots carefully and cut them in pieces. Any part of an underground stem that has at least one eye or shoot apparent should be capable of growing by itself. (See figure 3.) After cutting the stems, leave them in a cool spot for a few hours or overnight so that the cut place heals into a protective scab before replanting. Rhizomatous plants like iris are propagated by division in much the same way, but usually it is done right after flowering. Here you can see the fan of foliage, and each piece of rhizome with a fan is planted separately. Such new plantings should be watched so they are not too dry while new rooting is taking place, but don't let water puddle there.

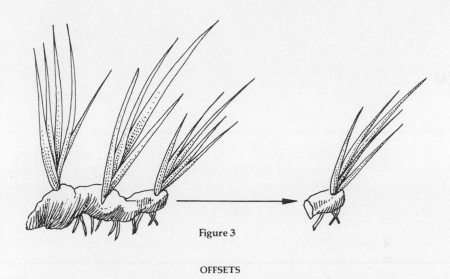

Figure 3

OFFSETS

This type of propagation is really just a facet of division. You do the dividing, but the plants have already been busy multiplying. Bulbous natives produce small bulblets next to the mother bulb, just as does a daffodil. Some form the new bulbs at the end of small roots. During dormancy any of these can be broken away and will grow on to maturity, sometimes faster for the lack of competition.

Herbaceous plants also produce a kind of offset. Helenium is one such. Around the original plant will be small new crowns of foliage as shown in figure 4. If cut from the rest with some roots

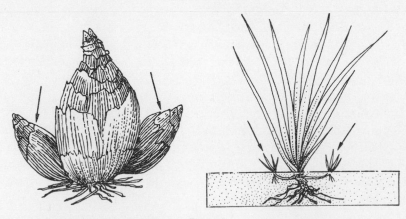

Figure 4

adhering, they will each form another plant. Perennials which produce many such growths are better if separated every few years, because they, too, may crowd each other out in the race for light, food, and moisture.

STOLONS

Some plants reproduce themselves by stolons (figure 5). These are stems around the periphery which have growing tips and vestiges of roots underground. If taken off the mother plant and potted and kept moist and shaded, these will often form a good, thrifty plant in a season or so. They have fewer feeder roots and are prone to drying, so they require more nursing than a regular division, which can usually just be replanted and left alone.

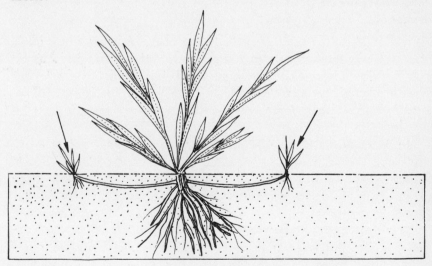

Figure 5

STEM CUTTINGS

Remember how your grandmother used to stick a piece of the tip of a rose shoot into the soil and cover it with a big glass jar to form another plant? I have done this with the stems of *Phlox* Miss Lingard in a moist shady place without benefit of the jar and had them root readily, but adequate humidity is important for this type of propagation. The ubiquitous plastic bag of today is easier than the glass jar. Take your stem cuttings in the spring and early summer after growth is well underway but before flowering begins. Cut the stem fairly close to the ground. Strip off the bottom two pairs of leaves carefully, nip off the growing shoot at a point so there are at least two pairs of leaves left on the stem. Dip the bottom end in rooting hormone, poke holes in your soil medium (sand and peat or perlite and peat are good mixtures), and insert the stem into the hole so the first pair of leaves is just above soil level. Firm the soil around the stem and water well. You can accommodate a group of cuttings in a 6-inch flower pot, since they need be only an inch or so apart. Now insert the whole pot into a large, clear plastic bag and fasten it at the top. Or make a frame atop the pot with a length of bent wire and tie a piece of clear plastic over it. Either way the pot is sealed inside the plastic. Place pots in a shaded spot. Usually they will not need any further watering, but do check them for moisture from time to time. (See figure 6.)

The only worry with such cuttings is that they may get mildew. The closed bag keeps the humidity high inside, and this is a prime environment for molds to develop. Initially, the soil should be damp but not wet; if you add too much water in the beginning, leave the bag open for a day until the surface feels just damp. For the first week check daily. If there is a high buildup of moisture film on the inside of the plastic, open it for an hour or so each day until you have allowed enough water vapor to escape so that the cuttings are in a moist-but-not-wet little world of their own. After a bit of practice you get so you are adept at guessing how much moisture is needed.

In a few weeks to a few months you may notice new growth appearing, an indication that the stems have rooted. The plants are then transplanted into pots just as carefully as you would little seedlings. They are best taken through their first winter either in a cold frame or with the pots buried to their rims in your protected nursery area.

You can use grandma's glass-jar technique instead if you wish. In that case leave the cuttings under the glass for the winter. Make sure all such procedures are done in spots where there is no sun. Even winter sun striking the glass jar will raise the temperature inside to a point where the plants within will cook.

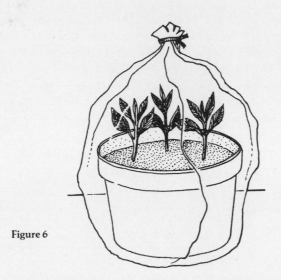

Figure 6

The glass terrarium, now undergoing a revival, is a fine place to root some cuttings. Any large container, even a fish bowl, can be utilized if you can give it a fairly close-fitting cover to keep in moisture and thus maintain humidity. Such a technique might be used inside for some rarity like trailing arbutus that you especially want to keep a good eye on. Mix the proper soil medium according to the acidity requirements of the plant in question and put the stem cuttings in it. Keep away from intense heat and strong sunlight and just let nature take its course inside the miniature world you have created. By adding a bit of water from time to time, you can keep slow-growing plants nearly a whole year this way. Time faster-growing species so they will be ready for spring planting outside by starting them late in the previous fall. Depending on how good a root system has developed, such plants are either ready to go right into the garden or require preliminary potting until there are enough roots for them to fend for themselves.

ROOT CUTTINGS

Some plants, particularly those with thick tuberous roots, like the butterflyweed, can be propagated with root cuttings. This process is best done in spring. Cut pieces of healthy root about two inches long. Use a mixture of coarse sand and peat or vermiculite and peat. Usually inserting the cuttings into a pot vertically, as in figure 7, works better than horizontally; but if one fails, try the other. Since there is no green top, the need for humidity, such as with stem cuttings, is not as great. Keep the containers or the bed moist—but not wet—until new shoots indicate new plants. Then transplant and winter over as with stem cuttings. You can also initiate the process in the fall, winter the pots in a cold frame, and expect new plants in spring.

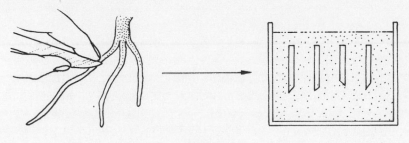

Figure 7

CORMOUS CUTTINGS

Plants like many liatris, which spring from a corm rather than a bulb, are propagated like potatoes. Dig up the mother plant in early spring and cut the corm into pieces so that each has a growing eye (figure 8). Let the pieces dry in a shady place for a few hours, then replant with the eye up in rows in the garden or in pots of loam. Frankly, this is not always successful, and I would forbear so treating a healthy cormous plant unless there is some special reason for wanting its increase. Sometimes a small corm forms along the edge or the top of the larger one. This is easier to remove and safer than radical surgery. Treating the cut surfaces with disinfectant is often suggested.

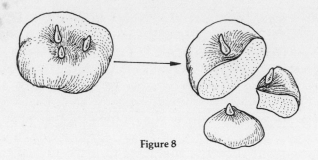

Figure 8

SCALES AND BULBILS

Lilies are true bulbs, but rather than being made up of concentric layers of tissue, as is the onion, they consist of many separate scales. You can increase them by treating the individual scales much like a seed. If you remove a few scales from the mother bulb while it is dormant, it will continue to bloom as before. (See figure 9.) The tiny bulbils that form along the stems of some plants are also best treated as seeds. It may take more than one season before any plants show, but just keep the container safe and watered in dry weather to see what happens.

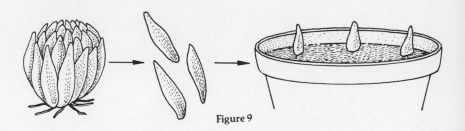

Figure 9

Conclusion

Perhaps because the word *propagation* sounds so formal, many gardeners do not see themselves as practitioners, although sowing a marigold seed is a form of it. As anyone who has done much propagating will tell you, it has a fascination and a satisfaction all its own. A plant you have raised yourself is somewhat like a child;

you cannot escape some feeling of pride when it does well. And as with children, it usually reflects the kind of care you gave it. Saying someone has a green thumb is just another way of saying that its owner takes cognizance of the needs of plants under his or her dominion. Like children, plants must be fed and watered, protected from hostile elements, and given various other kinds of tender loving care.

What makes the propagation of American natives even more intriguing is that it is a field still only lightly understood by many. At Bowman's Hill we have a saying that no colony of plants can be considered established until it has begun to reproduce itself. Soil acidity as well as the proper amounts of sun, water, and even bacterial action may all be factors. Nevertheless, the plants in this book are not particularly hard to propagate. But none of them will have a safe place in history until the home gardener has begun to increase them. Only in our gardens will they be safe, for the march of man is daily decreasing the wild stands.

PART II
100 Native American Perennials for Culture

5
Plants for Sunny Places

Essentially the plants in this section want nearly a full day of sunshine. Without it they straggle untidily, and bloom may be sparse. Many are plants of the prairies or the open fields. Some grow naturally along the edges of marshes or streams but will adapt to the garden. A few came originally from sandy, almost desertlike savannahs. Thus you may have to make allowances for more or less moisture when placing these plants in garden situations, but the common ingredient of lots of sun affects all.

Some species of genera more associated either with shade or with moisture are also sun-lovers or want partial sun. Use the Index to find:

Allium sp.
Chelone sp.
Hibiscus sp.
Houstonia sp.
Iris missouriensis
Lobelia siphilitica
Mertensia virginica

Nelumbo pentapetala
Nuphar sp.
Nymphaea sp.
Sanguisorba canadensis
Sedum sp.
Sisyrinchium sp.
Thalictrum sp.

Blue-Dogbane (*Amsonia tabernaemontana*)

FAMILY: Dogbane (*Apocynaceae*).
OTHER NICKNAMES: Willow amsonia, blue-star-of-Texas.
HABITAT: Any soil; sunny to half shady spots, often quite moist.
DESCRIPTION: Terminal clusters of small pale blue flowers; neat fountain of foliage turns yellow in fall; 2 to 3 ft. tall.
BLOOM PERIOD: Spring.
OUTSTANDING FEATURES: Dainty flowers, fall foliage.
NATURAL RANGE: New Jersey to Florida and Texas.
CULTURE: In drier situations this amsonia will flower just as well but usually remain shorter. Bloom is definitely better in full sun. It has a tendency to self-sow if seeds are allowed to develop, but the seedlings are easily weeded out when young. Each seedling makes a bushy clump after a few years. For this reason site amsonia in the garden so the graceful green wands act as a background for later-blooming plants. The fall coloring is quite outstanding. Darwin tulips are delightful as companions, since they bloom at the same time and provide a fine contrast. This amsonia is cultivated at least as far north as Massachusetts. If the first flowers are removed as they wither, secondary bloom occurs, but it is never as prolific as the first burst. The foliage is never bothered by insects or disease.
RELATED SPECIES: *A. ciliata* is a more southern species but perfectly hardy into the mid-Atlantic states. Its flower clusters are not as large, and it often grows to 4 or 5 ft. I consider it too big a plant for most gardens; the expanding foliage occupies more space than it is worth as the summer advances.
PROPAGATION: Easy from seed; divisions of mature plants in spring.

Blue-Dogbane (*Amsonia tabernaemontana*)

Pearly Everlasting (*Anaphalis margaritacea*)

FAMILY: Daisy (*Compositae*).
OTHER NICKNAMES: Life-everlasting, immortelle.
HABITAT: Takes poor, thin soil; any well-drained sunny spot.
DESCRIPTION: Makes a bushy plant with heads of small silvery white daisies and silvery green leaves; about 2 ft. tall.
BLOOM PERIOD: Late summer.
OUTSTANDING FEATURES: Silvery foliage and flowers make an interesting contrast with bright fall colors in rest of garden; if flowers are picked before maturity, they last many years in dried arrangements.
NATURAL RANGE: Newfoundland to Alaska; south to New York, Minnesota, South Dakota, Colorado and California, mostly in the mountains.
CULTURE: In the garden the only thing you need do for this plant is to make sure it has plenty of sun in a dryish spot. Its fluffy heads are indispensable to anyone who works with dried flowers. If gathered early, they retain more of a whitish shade. Later harvests tend to cream. Eventually the tiny seeds are dispersed by the wind, and only the outer row of bracts is left, but even this is useful as a dried flower although not as full as the less developed heads. For drying, pick with long stems, gather into bunches and hang upside down in a darkish, dry spot until the leaves and flowers are completely dry. They then may be stored indefinitely. Pearly everlasting also takes floral spray very nicely, so that you can make yourself raw materials in any number of colors in addition to the natural hue.
RELATED SPECIES: In Pennsylvania at least many of the pearly everlastings that decorate roadsides in northern parts of the state are annual or biennial forms of gnaphalium. Its flowers are similar to those of anaphalis and equally useful for drying, but some plants must be left to self-sow every year, so do not cut them all for early drying before the seeds mature. Also you will find seedlings in odd spots that may alter your garden design. Try to obtain the perennial instead.
PROPAGATION: By seed; perennials by division in spring.

Pearly Everlasting (*Anaphalis margaritacea*)

Pasque-Flower (*Anemone patens*)

FAMILY: Buttercup (*Ranunculaceae*).

OTHER NICKNAMES: Prairie smoke, windflower, wild-crocus, April fools, hartshorn-plant.

HABITAT: Well-drained loam; nearly full sun.

DESCRIPTION: Chalices 2 in. across, usually purple but sometimes white, on hairy stems 4 to 8 in. high; finely cut basal foliage.

BLOOM PERIOD: Early spring.

OUTSTANDING FEATURE: A striking flower for the garden foreground.

NATURAL RANGE: Arctic, northwest America; south to Michigan, Illinois, Missouri, Texas, New Mexico, Utah, and Washington.

CULTURE: This bright American from the Great Plains should be in every garden as a companion to daffodils or early tulips. The basal foliage develops after flowering and stays fresh and green all summer, eventually covering a good square foot. As the feathery seed plumes mature, the stems elongate. Goldfinches are reputedly very fond of the seed. Smart gardeners pick the heads before quite ripe and use them as delightful accents in dried bouquets. Fields full of seed heads inspired the name prairie smoke. Actually our American pasque-flower is considered *A. patens* var. *wolfganiana*, very closely related to the European form. Coming as it does from the far north, it is rock hardy. In the softer climate of my garden it does not seem to mind a little shade from nearby plants, and it gets whatever watering the rest of the garden receives in dry periods without seeming to care. Indeed, the foliage becomes quite lush and decorative as summer progresses. Never plant it in low spots where it will get excessive moisture, however. Rock gardeners are especially fond of these anemones, but there is no reason not to put them in any site with good drainage.

RECOMMENDED SELECTION: The white form is a knockout with early red tulips.

RELATED SPECIES: *A. occidentalis* of the western mountains often has white flowers. The various wood anemones (*A. virginiana*, *A. canadensis*, etc.) of the eastern woodlands grow from creeping rootstocks and are too invasive for most gardens but nice in large woodlands.

PROPAGATION: From seed; division of plants in spring. Pieces of the fleshy roots also form plants.

Pasque-Flower (*Anemone patens*)

Butterflyweed (*Asclepias tuberosa*)

FAMILY: Milkweed (*Asclepidaceae*).

OTHER NICKNAMES: Pleurisy-root, yellow milkweed, chigger-flower.

HABITAT: Takes thin, poor soil; sunny well-drained spots.

DESCRIPTION: Large flat umbels of small flowers ranging from bright yellow to reddish orange but mostly orange; 1 to 3 ft. high.

BLOOM PERIOD: Late spring and summer.

OUTSTANDING FEATURES: A bright summer decorative; plants practically indestructible once they get a good root system.

NATURAL RANGE: Ontario to Minnesota and Colorado; south to Florida, Texas, and Arizona.

CULTURE: Easily started from seed, butterflyweed makes good-sized clumps in time. While perfectly hardy, the first-year seedling roots are susceptible to heaving; mulch well and check frequently during the winter. Once it has put in a good root system, you need not worry. Transplant only small sizes for best results. The yellow and red shades are much rarer and much sought after by wild-flower enthusiasts. There will be some variation in color from any packet of seed. There is also a difference in when the flowers are produced. Those in my garden bloom in May, my neighbor's in August. In the wild this plant grows in the thinnest, poorest soil. Given better accommodations in the garden, it tends to grow taller but never needs staking. The flowers may be pressed or dried and retain their brilliance quite well. Seedpods are used in dried arrangements. So far no one has selected for color or named any cultivars that I know of.

RELATED SPECIES: Although there are many other milkweeds, the only other one really worth garden space is *A. incarnata* (swamp milkweed), which has pinkish flowers on 2- to 4-ft. stems. It will grow in quite wet situations. The common milkweed (*A. syriaca*) attracts butterflies even more than its orange cousin. If you have a handy field, it is quite decorative in flower, and its pods when gathered green are very useful in craft work. Its wandering roots, however, are a nuisance in the garden itself.

PROPAGATION: Easy from seed; by root cuttings in late spring.

Butterflyweed (*Asclepias tuberosa*)

Stiff-Leaved Aster (*Aster linariifolius*)

FAMILY: Daisy (*Compositae*).

OTHER NICKNAMES: Savory-leaf, bristly or sandpaper aster, pine-starwort.

HABITAT: Well-drained, somewhat acid soil; full sun.

DESCRIPTION: Lavender "daisies" about an inch wide with yellow central disks are borne on stiff-branched stems from 6 to 18 in. high; there is an early basal tuft of foliage.

BLOOM PERIOD: August to hard frost.

OUTSTANDING FEATURES: A neat plant to add late-season color to the foreground; good for rock gardens.

NATURAL RANGE: New Brunswick to Quebec and Minnesota; south to Florida and Texas.

CULTURE: This plant needs no pampering other than to make sure it has a spot with good drainage and full sun. Unlike so many of its cousins, it is not a spreader and never grows untidy or floppy, nor does it demand frequent division to stay healthy. Under most circumstances it makes a tidy mound about a foot high at bloom time. If it is sheared lightly in early summer before the buds form, it will give more compact bloom.

RECOMMENDED HYBRIDS: Despite fancy advertising about English asters, the famous Michaelmas daisies are actually hybrids of our native asters. There are many named cultivars in white, pink, and blue; heights range between 3 and 4 ft. There is also a race of named dwarf Pacific coast asters that stay around a foot tall and have the same range of hues. For best flowering both types must be divided in the spring every few years.

RELATED SPECIES: There are literally dozens of native asters, many too weedy to allow into the garden proper. A few are worth cultivating for special purposes. *A. conspicuous* from the west coast and *A. cordifolius* of the eastern woodlands are great in light shade. Both are 2 ft. high, have blue flowers, and are often called woodland asters. *A. puniceus* (swamp aster) grows in wet places and can reach 8 ft. with flowers ranging from white through many blues and even pink. Easiest to find in the catalogs is *A. novae-angliae* (New England aster), which varies from 3 to 6 ft. and is usually a rich purple although there is color variation in the wild. If you have a moist meadow, it is very flashy in late fall, but the hybrids are better for gardens.

PROPAGATION: Division in spring. Seedlings can be variable in habit of growth and bloom.

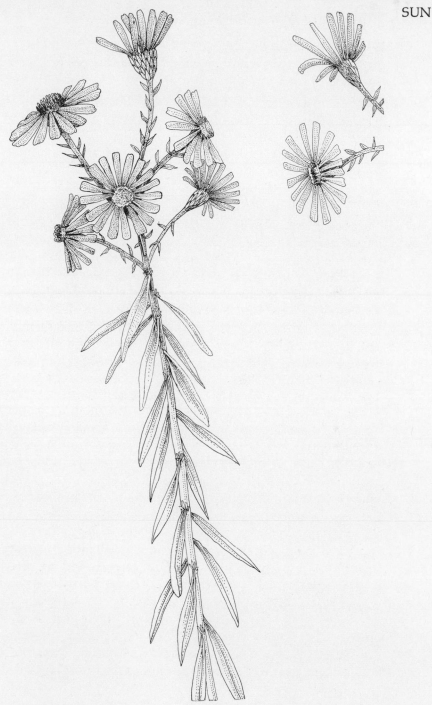

Stiff-Leaved Aster (*Aster linariifolius*)

Blue False-Indigo (*Baptisia australis*)

FAMILY: Pea (*Leguminosae*).
OTHER NICKNAME: Wild-indigo.
HABITAT: Well-drained loam; full sun.
DESCRIPTION: Erect racemes of dark blue pea flowers 3 to 4 ft. high; bluish green leaves attractive all summer.
BLOOM PERIOD: Late spring.
OUTSTANDING FEATURES: Long-lived, insect-free, lush foliage.
NATURAL RANGE: Pennsylvania to Georgia, West Virginia, Indiana, and Kentucky.
CULTURE: Although the long sprays of flowers are interesting in their season, this baptisia's main garden value is as a foliage plant. The clean green leaves make a fine foil for later flowers. In time it can even be used as a short deciduous hedge, because each plant becomes a strong clump after a few years. You are advised to plan carefully before adding it to the garden. The root system becomes so extensive that an old plant cannot be easily moved. Set seedlings in their permanent home by the second spring for best results. In time each will cover an area several feet in diameter with gracefully arching foliage. This plant will put up with a little filtered shade, but growth will not be as exuberant. Because it is a legume, baptisia will grow moderately well even in poor soil, and it has much to recommend itself as a plant to hold banks because of its extensive root system. In late summer the big seedpods turn black. Either plain or gilded, they are popular for dried arrangements. If desired for this use, cut the seedpods on long stems in early fall before they become too weathered. Place upright in containers in a dry, well-ventilated spot until needed.
RECOMMENDED HYBRIDS: From time to time seed of hybrids is offered, mostly in yellow, bronze, and violet shades.
RELATED SPECIES: *B. tinctoria* will grow in poor, dry soil and is sometimes suggested as an anti-erosion plant, but its summertime yellow flowers are small and too insignificant for garden use. *B. leucantha*, with white flowers, blooms later than *B. australis*, but is too tall and rangy for most gardens. *B. bracteata* is creamy, seldom tops 2 ft. and has drooping racemes. All of these species have more northerly ranges than their blue cousin, but the latter is hardy enough to try anywhere in the United States and southern Canada.
PROPAGATION: Easy from seed; by division in spring.

Blue False-Indigo (*Baptisia australis*)

Mariposa-Lily (*Calochortus venustus*)

FAMILY: Lily (*Liliaceae*).
OTHER NICKNAME: Butterfly-tulip.
HABITAT: Very well-drained, thin, gritty soil; full sun.
DESCRIPTION: Upright cups on thin stems to 2 ft.; colors are variable: white, yellow, purple, or rose, usually with a blotch on each petal and intricate markings in the center.
BLOOM PERIOD: Early summer.
OUTSTANDING FEATURES: Incredibly beautiful but difficult in east.
NATURAL RANGE: California.
CULTURE: Gardeners in states with normal or high rainfall will not find any of this clan easy to keep. It encompasses flowers so very magnificent, however, that they are worth trying. There are more than fifty species from the Pacific and western states. Native habitats are widely varied, but this advice seems to work best: plant bulbs late in fall so no early growth will take place, in a south-facing spot with absolutely perfect drainage. Mulch after frost to prevent heaving. Make sure plants have water during and just after flowering, then keep as dry as possible during summer and fall dormancy. Some experts lift them after the foliage matures to ensure this. A raised bed can be a help. Most calochortus bulbs offered are a mixture, but this species is apt to be included. Most are cold-hardy but cannot take winter thawing or summer wet. Tall ones need staking or a nearby supporting plant to display the flowers best.
RECOMMENDED SELECTION: The El Dorado strain is available.
RELATED SPECIES: *Mariposa* is Spanish for *butterfly*; most of the calochortus included in that general group are tall and upright. There are other dwarf calochortus with hairs lining the interiors which are called cat's-ears, owl's-ears, or star-tulips. An even more beautiful group are variously known as fairy-lanterns, globe-tulips, or satin-bells. These have pendulous flowers and an ethereal quality. As a group they make a better garden picture because they do not sprawl quite as much, but bulbs are harder to find.
PROPAGATION: By seed, but difficult, and don't expect flowering for some years; in theory by offsets, but be satisfied if you can just keep them alive. A few species bear bulbils in the leaf axils.

Mariposa-Lily (*Calochortus venustus*)

Harebell (*Campanula rotundifolia*)

FAMILY: Bluebell (*Campanulaceae*).

OTHER NICKNAMES: Bluebells of Scotland, bellflower, varied-leaf bluebell.

HABITAT: Well-drained, humusy soil; sun.

DESCRIPTION: Small, nodding, blue bells on wiry stems 6 to 18 in. high, but usually averaging about 1 ft.

BLOOM PERIOD: Summer.

OUTSTANDING FEATURES: A long-blooming dainty blue note for slopes and rock gardens.

NATURAL RANGE: Northern North America as well as northern Eurasia.

CULTURE: Good drainage is imperative if this plant is to do well, but in niches of the rock garden which approximate its natural home on cliffs, it may prove too happy, this because it spreads by underground stems and thus may take over space saved for rarer plants. In warmer climates give some shade for best results and do not let it want for water during the summer. I have read that harebells are found in moist meadows in the northern states, but in the Philadelphia area it does very nicely in humusy gardens. The nickname varied-leaf bluebell is given because stem leaves are narrow while the basal foliage consists of round leaves. The tuft of basal foliage is decorative in the winter garden but disappears during summer bloom. Expect color variation in different strains. There are many shades of blue to purple plus rare whites.

RELATED SPECIES: *C. petiolata* is a similar western species. About 14 in. high, it is reputedly a rugged plant that blooms all summer. *C. divaricata* (North Carolina harebell) is an even daintier species. Its tiny light-blue bells are hardly the size of a pencil eraser and borne in open arching panicles about 15 in. high. In the wild this is found in both sun and part shade, but farther north give it full sun. Even then, it may not prove long-lived, but it is worth trying because of its daintiness and very long summer blossoming. Never plant *C. rapunculoides*, a European bellflower that has naturalized widely in the northeast; it spreads far too fast for any garden.

PROPAGATION: By seed; by division in spring.

Harebell (*Campanula rotundifolia*)

Tickseed (*Coreopsis verticillata*)

FAMILY: Daisy (*Compositae*).

OTHER NICKNAMES: Thread-leaved coreopsis, whorled tickseed, pot-of-gold.

HABITAT: Almost any dry soil; sun.

DESCRIPTION: Small yellow daisies on wiry stems 1 to 3 ft. high; foliage somewhat ferny.

BLOOM PERIOD: All summer and fall.

OUTSTANDING FEATURES: A creeping plant for hot, difficult places.

NATURAL RANGE: Maryland to Florida, Alabama, and Arkansas.

CULTURE: It would be unwise to plant this native in a garden where rare species are being encouraged, but for a very hot, sunny, dry spot it is hard to beat and seems hardy much farther north than its natural range. Shear the old seed heads from time to time during the summer to help the plants bloom until hard frost. In too rich a loam this coreopsis either spreads too quickly by creeping stolons or peters out from too much kindness. Where soil is thin, it also tends to stay shorter, acting more like a groundcover.

RECOMMENDED HYBRIDS AND SELECTIONS: Golden Shower is a selected form of *C. verticillata*. Several excellent named dwarf coreopsis are in the trade: Baby Sun, Goldfink, Canarybird. There are also named selections of *C. lanceolata*, which is an erect 2 ft. species; Baby Gold, Brown Eyes, Sunburst (semidouble), Gold Coin, Mayfield Giant, and Golden Wheel are all available.

RELATED SPECIES: A few wildflower houses carry *C. lanceolata* itself, and it is a very hardy, undemanding source of good long-stemmed yellow flowers for cutting. *C. rosea* is a creeping, rather rare 2 ft. pink species found in wet sandy spots along the eastern coast; it has a dwarf form much prized by rock gardeners. *C. auriculata* can go to 18 in., has small yellow flowers, and spreads by stoloniferous roots; its dwarf form (*nana*) bears orange yellow blossoms and has less spreading tendencies. *C. grandiflora* can reach 30 in. but sprawls. Some other species grow much taller, better for fields than gardens. *C. tripteris* with soft lemon rays and a brownish disk reaches 6 ft. and is the best. *C. maritima* (sea-dahlia) is a 3-ft. southern California coastal species not hardy in northern winters.

PROPAGATION: Species by seed; others by division in spring.

Tickseed (*Coreopsis verticillata*)

Wild Larkspur (*Delphinium tricorne*)

FAMILY: Buttercup (*Ranunculaceae*).
OTHER NICKNAMES: Rock or dwarf larkspur, staggerweed.
HABITAT: Well-drained neutral to limy soil; at least half sun.
DESCRIPTION: Small heads of blue, violet, or white flowers on stems 1 to 2 ft. high; finely cut foliage.
BLOOM PERIOD: Spring.
OUTSTANDING FEATURES: The first delphinium to blossom and a delicate gem for rock garden or edge of a woodsy site.
NATURAL RANGE: Pennsylvania to Minnesota and Nebraska; south to Georgia, Alabama, Arkansas, and Oklahoma.
CULTURE: It is a shame no selection has yet been done on this relative of the garden delphinium. How lovely it would be to have colonies of all one color. Although often considered a plant of the woods, it must have sunshine to bloom well. If planted on the fringes of a deciduous woodland, this wild larkspur will get sufficient light because it does all its growing early in the season. Bloom is usually on stems near 12 in. They then elongate while producing seed. Soon thereafter the plants go completely dormant; mark their site well lest you disturb the tuberous roots inadvertently. In a woodland garden where the soil is on the acid side, mulch with marble chips.
RELATED SPECIES: *D. carolinianum* is much similar but blooms a month later. The 5-ft. *D. exaltatum* extends the season into the summer. Both these species prefer slightly acid soil. You must place them more carefully because they, too, need at least half a day of sunshine to flower well. For northern gardens *D. glaucum*, which is found in Alaska, might be a better choice. *D. menziesi* (sometimes listed as *D. nelsoni*) is a western form much similar in habit and bloom to the eastern dwarf species. *D. nudicaule* is a red-and-yellow species from California which can sometimes survive in more northern gardens if given a very dry, protected spot. *D. cardinale* is also red, but its absolute need for summer dryness is difficult for easterners to fulfill. *D. trollifolium* from Oregon has a long raceme of small blue flowers.
PROPAGATION: By seed; by division when dormant.

Wild Larkspur (*Delphinium tricorne*)

Purple Coneflower (*Echinacea purpurea*)

FAMILY: Daisy (*Compositae*).

OTHER NICKNAME: Purple rudbeckia.

HABITAT: Almost any well-drained soil; full sun.

DESCRIPTION: Large, somewhat coarse flowers with a striking bronzy-brown disk of florets surrounded by ray flowers of purple on stems 2 to 4 ft. tall.

BLOOM PERIOD: Summer.

OUTSTANDING FEATURES: Undemanding daisies for summer garden.

NATURAL RANGE: Virginia to Michigan, Illinois, and Iowa; south to Georgia, and Louisiana.

CULTURE: Although the black-eyed Susan (*Rudbeckia hirta*) is a beloved American flower, it is usually biennial in habit, so I suggest this near cousin for garden use. One of the named cultivars will give the same effect as the brown-and-yellow favorite of the fields but will prove a better garden inhabitant. Nomenclature in the family is mixed anyway, and it is likely some of the hybrids contain genes from both genera. *E. purpurea* takes a year or so to develop into much of a clump from seed. Remove old flower heads before seed forms to encourage long blooming. These flowers are perfectly hardy in northern gardens.

RECOMMENDED HYBRIDS: Many of the named cultivars in nursery catalogs are of European origin, but their bloodlines are strictly American. They may be listed either as rudbeckias or as echinaceas. Bright Star, Robert Bloom, and The King all have ray flowers in the maroon or rose spectrum and to my eye are better colors than the species. White Lustre has cones more on the yellow side and white rays. Gold Sturm (Storm) or Orange Bedder resemble the black-eyed Susan. Old-time gardeners all had Golden Glow, a double form of *R. laciniata* (the cutleaf coneflower) that made a fine cut flower but often grew at least 6 ft. tall and spread rapidly. There is now a dwarf form called Gold Quelle, which seldom tops 30 in. and is advertised as not being invasive. Double Gold is an All-America winner growing about 3 ft. Irish Eyes has a green cone and is somewhat shorter but short-lived. The gloriosa daisies of the catalogs are closely related. They come in yellows and mahogany, some plain, some bicolored; but not all are reliably perennial.

PROPAGATION: By seed for species; cultivars by division in spring.

Purple Coneflower (*Echinacea purpurea*)

Mistflower (*Eupatorium coelestinum*)

FAMILY: Daisy (*Compositae*).

OTHER NICKNAMES: Hardy ageratum, blue boneset, hemp agrimony.

HABITAT: Almost any soil; sun or partial shade; likes moisture.

DESCRIPTION: Flat-topped clusters of soft fluffy violet-blue flowers 3 to 4 ft. tall.

BLOOM PERIOD: Late summer and fall.

OUTSTANDING FEATURE: Good blue for the late garden.

NATURAL RANGE: New Jersey to Illinois and Kansas; south to Florida and Texas.

CULTURE: An undemanding plant, the mistflower should be in every garden. The fine blue it adds to the last months of the garden year contrasts delightfully with the bright hues of chrysanthemums, and it cuts well for bouquets, too. In damp situations this eupatorium spreads very quickly by stoloniferous roots, but in the drier garden it is easier to control and usually shorter of stature, too. Remember that it is late appearing in spring, so don't give up on it too soon. In the dry garden there may well be some winterkill; but this also helps to keep it from spreading too quickly. In the northern states it is better grown in a wetter soil. If the old flowers are removed, mistflower continues to put forth new bloom for a long time, even until hard frost if you are faithful about the deheading.

RECOMMENDED SELECTION: Wayside Variety is a somewhat dwarfer form than the type.

RELATED SPECIES: The various lilac or purple eupatoriums are often called Joe-Pye-weed. As with white boneset (*E. perfoliatum*), they are too tall and rough for the ordinary garden. For waste swampy areas, however, they provide fine color in late summer. The 4- to 10-ft. *E. purpureum* is one of the best. A recommended white eupatorium is described in the chapter on flowers for shade.

PROPAGATION: Easy from seed; more commonly by division in late spring.

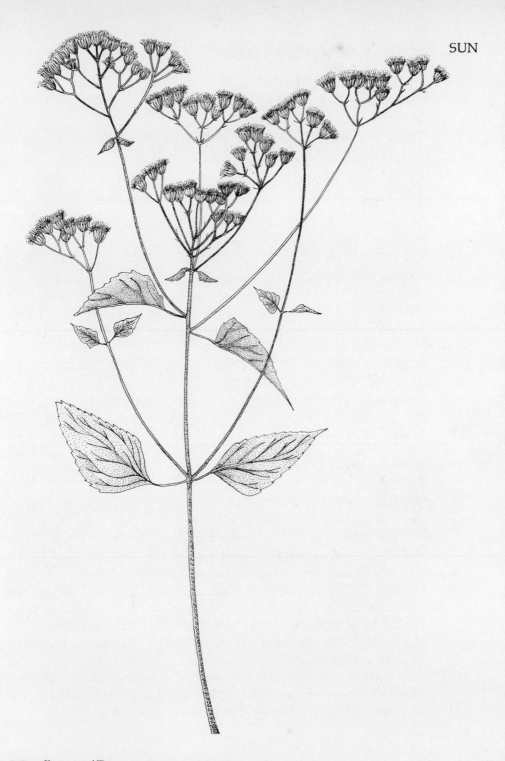

Mistflower (*Eupatorium coelestinum*)

Yellow Bell (*Fritillaria pudica*)

FAMILY: Lily (*Liliaceae*).
OTHER NICKNAMES: Yellow fritillary, Indian-rice, rice-root.
HABITAT: Well-drained loam; full sun.
DESCRIPTION: Nodding yellow bells, often tinged brownish purple, on stems 6 to 8 in. long; erect basal leaves.
BLOOM PERIOD: Spring.
OUTSTANDING FEATURE: A dainty rarity for rock garden or dry niche.
NATURAL RANGE: British Columbia to California and New Mexico.
CULTURE: There are a number of lovely little bulbous plants from the western states in this genus, but most of them are hard to obtain and difficult to cultivate in eastern gardens. While some come from winter-free parts of California, others are mountain dwellers from areas where frost comes early and leaves late. Many eastern gardeners experience a problem with alternate freezing and thawing plus an overabundance of rain at the wrong times. In any case, these plants are well worth further investigation by the gardener who wants something different. All should be well mulched to prevent heaving. *F. pudica* is one of the easier species. For best effect plant it in a group because it is a rather diminutive beauty. You do not want it to be overlooked. Choose a spot where there is not the slightest chance of standing water ever. If you have a slope, so much the better. Never give it any extra water in the summertime.
RELATED SPECIES: Red bells or scarlet fritillary (*F. recurva*)—sometimes also called mission bells—may bear its scarlet flowers 24 in. high. They come a bit later in the spring, and this mountaineer does best with afternoon shade. The chocolate lily (*F. camschatcensis*) grows in Alaska and Siberia so is certainly hardy enough. Its brownish purple bells are more open and lilylike and on stems about 1 ft. tall. In gardens south of its natural range it should have humusy soil in light shade and the coolest spot you can find. There are other native fritillaries, but most are recommended for experts only. Start with the easy ones first.
PROPAGATION: By seed, but it will take some time. In addition mature bulbs produce small bulblets like grains of rice, which may be removed after the foliage dies down in summer.

Yellow Bell (*Fritillaria pudica*)

Sneezeweed (*Helenium autumnale*)

FAMILY: Daisy (*Compositae*).

OTHER NICKNAMES: Helen's flower, swamp sunflower.

HABITAT: Rich loam; full sun; give extra water in summer.

DESCRIPTION: Heads of small yellow daisies on stout stems that branch toward the top and can reach 6 ft.; basal rosettes are evergreen where winters are not too harsh.

BLOOM PERIOD: Late summer.

OUTSTANDING FEATURE: A good tall source of late summer color.

NATURAL RANGE: Quebec to Minnesota and Nebraska; south to Florida and Arizona.

CULTURE: Although found in dampish spots in the wild, helenium adapts very well to the ordinary garden, especially if there is a lowish spot. You can tailor the site by making a slight depression when you plant the helenium. During periods of drought give it a good hosing. It is particularly important to see that it gets extra water in midsummer to encourage good flowering. The main drawback to the true species is that it may grow too tall for the smaller garden. Nipping off the growing tips in the spring helps create bushier, shorter plants. Every few years it is also advisable to cut the mother plant apart in the spring to keep it thrifty. The common name should warn allergy sufferers not to bring sneezeweed or its selections and hybrids into the house.

RECOMMENDED HYBRIDS AND SELECTIONS: There are some excellent selected varieties and hybrids that are more useful for the home gardener. *H. pumilum magnificum* Sunburst grows to about 15 in. and is very bushy, making a mound of yellow. Also yellow but to 3 ft. is Butterpat. Bruno, Copper Spray, Crimson Beauty, Gypsy, Chippersfield Orange, Copelia, Moorheim Beauty, and Wyndley exhibit various shades of red and orange and range from 2 to 4 ft. tall. The central disks of some are very dark, making a nice contrast both in the garden and for cutting.

RELATED SPECIES: *H. nudiflorum* (purple-head sneezeweed) has large ball-shaped brownish heads and yellow rays and seldom grows taller than 3 ft. Bitterweed (*H. amarum*) is a much slenderer species but well branched and about 2 ft. tall. I would love to have *H. hoopesi* from the Rockies, which ranges from 2 to 3 ft. and blooms earlier.

PROPAGATION: By seed for species; hybrids and species by division in spring.

Sneezeweed (*Helenium autumnale*)

Ox-Eye (*Heliopsis helianthoides*)

FAMILY: Daisy (*Compositae*).
OTHER NICKNAMES: False sunflower, sun glory, orange sunflower.
HABITAT: Almost any soil; full sun.
DESCRIPTION: Bright yellow daisies often 4 in. across on sturdy stems; plants are 3 to 5 ft. tall.
BLOOM PERIOD: Summer until frost.
OUTSTANDING FEATURE: Excellent for cutting.
NATURAL RANGE: Ontario to Minnesota; south to Florida, Texas, and New Mexico.
CULTURE: This undemanding plant is one of those pleasant rarities: a perennial which blooms well the first year from seed. It is much better for the flower garden than its near relatives, the sunflowers. The plants of heliopsis do not take as much room, and they are much more floriferous. Indeed, if the spent flowers are removed frequently, heliopsis will continuing producing new blossoms until hard frost. It will even flower in a partially shaded position. Bloom is best in good loam, but I have had plants do well even in rather stiff clay. The plants form clumps in time. During dry summers heliopsis must have extra water; at midday plants may even actually wilt. A harsh spray of water on the foliage also discourages aphids, which sometimes attack heliopsis in dry weather. No one who enjoys indoor bouquets should be without this gay daisy.
RECOMMENDED SELECTIONS AND HYBRIDS: Summer Sun has fairly double golden yellow flowers; *H. scabra incomparabilis* is orange yellow and usually at least semidouble; Golden Plume and Gold Greenheart are both double; Light of Loddon is a yellow single and Orange King another bright shade.
PROPAGATION: Easily from seed; by division in spring. Sometimes plants self-sow freely.

Ox-Eye (*Heliopsis helianthoides*)

Coral-Bell (*Heuchera sanguinea*)

FAMILY: Rockfoil (*Saxifragaceae*).

OTHER NICKNAME: Alumroot.

HABITAT: Well-drained, humusy soil; nearly full sun.

DESCRIPTION: Sprays of tiny bells in red, pink, or white on 1- to 2-ft. slender stems; mounds of evergreen foliage.

BLOOM PERIOD: Much of spring and summer.

OUTSTANDING FEATURES: Neat foliage would be interesting alone, but long blooming period is also a plus.

NATURAL RANGE: New Mexico and Arizona, but hardy in north.

CULTURE: Where summers are hot, these plants can take a little filtered shade, but they are essentially for sunny places. Although the flower stems can reach considerable height, the blossoms are so dainty that coral-bells are often used as foreground plantings. Such practice takes special advantage of the delightful foliage. These plants have been extensively bred both in America and in England with several other western species. The resulting hybrids are even better choices for the garden, since they are more floriferous and come in a wider range of colors. All make dainty fillers in bouquets and press well for craft work. Removing old flowers before seed can form definitely prolongs bloom. Winter wet adversely affects all heucheras, but they do like some humus in the soil. Every few years divide the big plants to prevent their crowding themselves out.

RECOMMENDED HYBRIDS: The Bressingham hybrids are a good seed strain, but some wonderful cultivars are available as plants from many nurseries: White Cloud, Queen of Hearts, June Bride, Chartreuse, Coral Mist, Snowflakes, Scarlet Sentinel, Fire Sprite, Rain of Fire.

RELATED SPECIES: *H. villosa* is a terrific southern species which is perfectly hardy at least to the Philadelphia area and wants nearly full sun. It bears sprays of tiny white bells on stems 15 in. high for a very long time in late summer above foliage that has pointed lobes rather than the round ones of the rest of the family. Toward fall these leaves turn bronze, just like the maples they resemble. *H. americana* grows wild up to eastern Canada. It will take more shade than the westerners, bears greenish bells in late spring, but is at best a very quiet sister in comparison with the others.

PROPAGATION: By seed; by division in spring. Stem cuttings broken from close to the crown root readily.

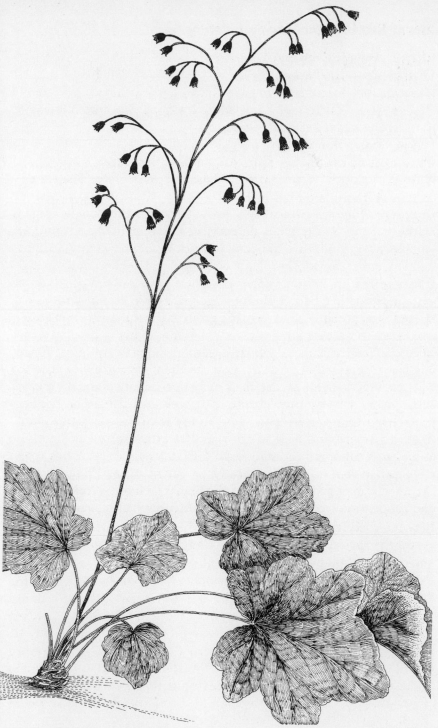

Coral-Bell (*Heuchera sanguinea*)

Spider-Lily (*Hymenocallis occidentalis*)

FAMILY: Amaryllis (*Amaryllidaceae*).
OTHER NICKNAME: Basketflower.
HABITAT: Rich loam; full sun.
DESCRIPTION: Clusters of large white fragrant flowers on stems 2 ft. tall; long straplike basal foliage.
BLOOM PERIOD: Summer.
OUTSTANDING FEATURE: A dramatic summer decorative.
NATURAL RANGE: Georgia to Alabama; north to Kentucky, Indiana, Illinois, and Missouri.
CULTURE: Only experiment will prove whether this lovely cousin of the ismene or Peruvian daffodil can winter in the ground at your locality. Bulbs are not easy to find, however, so it would be wise to start cautiously. Plant them several inches deep in the garden after all frost is gone and then gather them for winter storage inside before fall nights get cold. Leave as many roots on the bulbs as possible when you dig them in the fall, and store frost-free with some dirt adhering to the bulbs. This is precisely the culture given the ismene, which is native to South America. Once you have increased your stock, you can then leave a few outside to winter over. When you are ready to experiment, plant the bulbs about 6 in. deep and mulch the spot well and deeply as further protection. Our native spider-lily, to my mind, is a daintier plant than the ismene and well worth the little extra trouble of treating as a tender summer-blooming bulb if that is necessary. It has been wintered over outside successfully as far north as Philadelphia. During summer growth never let the plants lack for water. At least one application of a good houseplant fertilizer is also suggested.
RELATED SPECIES: *H. crassifolia* and *H. coronaria* are more southerly species and less hardy. They are found along streams and in coastal-plain marshes.
PROPAGATION: By offsets of the bulbs, which can be separated in the spring before planting.

Spider-Lily *(Hymenocallis occidentalis)*

Blazing-Star (*Liatris scariosa*)

FAMILY: Daisy (*Compositae*).
OTHER NICKNAMES: Button snake-root, gayfeather.
HABITAT: Not too rich well-drained soil; full sun; winter wet fatal.
DESCRIPTION: Purple or white fluffy disk flowers set along a spike 3 to 6 ft. tall; narrow leaves along stem.
BLOOM PERIOD: Summer into fall.
OUTSTANDING FEATURES: Tall, stately plant for late summer color.
NATURAL RANGE: Pennsylvania and West Virginia; south to Georgia and Mississippi.
CULTURE: It was hard to pick which liatris species to feature, especially since each hybridizes easily. All liatris are good garden plants. If you grow them from seed, you may well find there is considerable variation among the plants you get. Some may bloom earlier than others, some may branch along the main stem, and heights also vary widely. None can take wet soil, but to get good bloom they should be watered if the summer is dry. Grown from seed, they will take several years before they make a good-sized clump. Tallest varieties may need staking unless grown along with shrubs or other big plants that can help support them. If the liatris are placed in groups, they also tend to support each other. The flowering comes at a time when the garden needs a new accent. White varieties come true from seed, and I find them easier to work into the total garden picture, but the purple forms are more common, and they are a soft shade that does not really clash with other colors too badly. Bloom begins at the top, so in a bouquet you can clip off the old flowers and utilize the spike for a long time.
RECOMMENDED SELECTIONS AND HYBRIDS: Kobold and Silver Tips are two early blooming named cultivars that are seldom taller than 24 in. and thus never need staking. September Glory and White Spire are both tall.
RELATED SPECIES: *L. pycnostachya* is sometimes called cattail gayfeather and ranges from 3 to 5 ft. *L. spicata* is variable in height but forms very neat long spikes of flowers and will take a damper site than the others. *L. graminifolia* (grass-leaved liatris) is a slender form around 3 ft. tall.
PROPAGATION: By seed. Some tuberous types produce little tubers alongside the main one which can be pried off in early spring. Propagate also by stem cuttings in spring after growth has begun.

108

Blazing-Star (*Liatris scariosa*)

Canada Lily (*Lilium canadense*)

FAMILY: Lily (*Liliaceae*).

OTHER NICKNAMES: Wild yellow lily, meadow lily.

HABITAT: Rich neutral to moderately acid soil; partial sun; must not lack for moisture during growth period.

DESCRIPTION: Candelabras of nodding yellow or reddish bell-shaped flowers on stems 4 to 10 ft. tall.

BLOOM PERIOD: Early summer.

OUTSTANDING FEATURES: One of the easiest and hardiest, and certainly one of the loveliest, of our native lilies for garden use.

NATURAL RANGE: New Brunswick to Ontario and Minnesota; south to Missouri, Georgia, and Alabama.

CULTURE: All wildflower guides note that this lily is found in wet woods and meadows, so the innocent gardener may think it should go into a soggy spot. Unfortunately, those wild stands are paradoxical: they contain damp loam that is well-drained. To approximate this in the garden, use plenty of humus when preparing the site. Should spring and summer be dry, give extra water, but never put bulbs in a spot where water collects and stays. Better they be too dry than too wet. The rhizomatous bulbs are planted 6 in. deep. If conditions are to their liking, they will increase into a fine colony. A shallow-rooted groundcover and a mulch help keep the bulbs cool. Or place them behind a short shrub. Pick the site so that it gets half a day of good sun, preferably in the morning. Mice relish lily bulbs, and rabbits and deer eat foliage, so you may have to take preventive measures.

RECOMMENDED SELECTIONS AND HYBRIDS: So far there are no hybrids of eastern native lilies, but specialists offer *L. canadense editorum*, a vigorous red form; var. *flavum* has golden yellow bells spotted red; var. *rubrum* contains red shades. The fine Bellingham hybrids were made from crosses of western native lilies and range from soft yellow and creamy lavender through red. Named clones of these hybrids include Afterglow, Buttercup, Nightingale, Robin, San Gabriel, Shuksan, and Bunting.

RELATED SPECIES: Other eastern lilies worth trying in the garden include *L. michiganense*, *L. superbum*, and *L. michauxi*. The wood lily (*L. philadelphicum*) requires very acid soil. *L. kelloggi* and *L. pardalinum*, both westerners, are worth trying, too.

PROPAGATION: By seed; by scales; by offsets.

110

Canada Lily (*Lilium canadense*)

Bee-Balm (*Monarda didyma*)

FAMILY: Mint (*Labiatae*).

OTHER NICKNAMES: Bergamot, Oswego-tea, horse-mint, fragrant-balm.

HABITAT: Almost any soil, but likes moisture; sun.

DESCRIPTION: Heads studded with lipped bright red flowers on sturdy stems 3 to 4 ft. tall.

BLOOM PERIOD: Summer into fall, if heads are removed before seed forms.

OUTSTANDING FEATURE: Attractive to bees, butterflies, and hummingbirds.

NATURAL RANGE: New York to Michigan; south to Georgia and Mississippi.

CULTURE: The monardas are spreaders. On the edge of a field or a truly wild garden, this may not matter, but in the border their creeping roots will take over increasing amounts of territory unless the excess are removed from time to time. Division of large plants also keeps them healthier. They are most useful for spots too moist for other plants, but their long blooming period also makes them colorful choices for the ordinary garden, where they grow very well. Under drier conditions they usually do not spread as fast and are somewhat shorter than the maximum. While they will grow in a little shade, they tend to get floppy with too much shade. With enough sunshine, however, they stand straight without any need of staking. Some extra watering during dry summers is a good practice. If you buy the species monarda, expect some variation in the shades of red.

RECOMMENDED HYBRIDS AND SELECTIONS: There has been extensive selection and hybridizing of our two native monardas. In the small garden, one of these improved forms is probably the wiser choice if only because you will be sure of the color. By shopping around you can find monardas in pink, white, red, rose, purple, and mahogany. Many are named cultivars: Granite Pink, Cambridge Scarlet, Snow Maiden, Adam, Croftway Pink, Sunset, Salmon Queen. They are hardy at least into southern Canada.

RELATED SPECIES: *M. fistulosa* is a pink species found in drier areas and farther north than Oswego-tea, but otherwise similar.

PROPAGATION: By seed, but colors may be variable; by division in spring.

112

Bee-Balm (*Monarda didyma*)

Evening-Primrose (*Oenothera fruticosa*)

FAMILY: Evening-primrose (*Onagraceae*).
OTHER NICKNAME: Sundrops.
HABITAT: Thin, well-drained soil; full sun.
DESCRIPTION: Bright yellow flowers 2 in. across, borne in clusters on stems 1 to 2 ft. high; basal rosettes are evergreen in mid-Atlantic states area.
BLOOM PERIOD: Summer.
OUTSTANDING FEATURE: Bright decorative for dry areas.
NATURAL RANGE: New Hampshire to Michigan; south to Florida, Louisiana, and Oklahoma.
CULTURE: The promiscuous sex life of the oenotheras results in constant hybridizing. Because of this, plants you buy may not always be true to name. Often one believed to be perennial will act as a biennial. Nevertheless, they are a very bright addition to the sunny garden. Some very good selections have been made, especially in Europe, and these are probably better choices for the finicky gardener who can find them. If you have a dry spot where you just want some sunny color, plants bought under species names are good to start with. *O. fruticosa* spreads rapidly, but being shallow-rooted, unwanted plants are easily pulled out. It can take a little light shade. Gathered in early winter, the seed heads of most oenotheras are useful for dried arrangements.
RECOMMENDED HYBRIDS AND SELECTIONS: Yellow River is sometimes sold. Var. *youngi* is shorter and more floriferous than the type. There are some good hybrids of *O. tetragona:* Illumination, Fireworks, Highlight, and Riparia. Sometimes these are cataloged as *O. fyrverkeri* or *O. fraseri*.
RELATED SPECIES: *O. missouriensis* makes a spreading mound about 6 in. high with large flowers and is excellent for rock gardens or dry walls. *O. perennis* is a fine long-blooming, very dwarf species. *O. speciosa* has both white and rose forms. It may be listed as *O. mexicana* and is not always hardy far north. Before planting any evening-primrose, try to ascertain if it is perennial (although most biennials seed prolifically), then at which hours it blooms. Some species open only toward sunset. This habit can be interesting near a patio, and some flowers are deliciously fragrant, but of course these species do nothing to color a sunny daytime garden.
PROPAGATION: By seed; by division in spring.

Evening-Primrose (*Oenothera fruticosa*)

Prickly-Pear (*Opuntia compressa*)

FAMILY: Cactus (*Cactaceae*).

OTHER NAME: *O. compressa* is sometimes botanically designated as *O. humifusa*.

HABITAT: Very well-drained soil; full sun.

DESCRIPTION: Large yellow flowers and reddish fruits; odd fleshy, slightly branched joints instead of leaves are seldom higher than 6 in.

BLOOM PERIOD: Summer.

OUTSTANDING FEATURE: Something different for dry areas.

NATURAL RANGE: Ontario and Minnesota; south to South Carolina, Georgia, Alabama, Missouri, and Oklahoma.

CULTURE: There are nearly 300 opuntia species in either North or South America, but this is one of the hardiest. Many others are found in the west. These may have either pink or yellow blooms and local nicknames like bunny-ears, blind-pear, grizzly-bear cactus, or beavertail cactus. Winter cold is not nearly as important a killing factor for many as wetness in any season. *O. compressa* in my garden increases slowly in clay soil, but the addition of some sand or grit is often a wise measure to aid drainage. The joints root where they touch the ground. In fall the fruits, which are bigger than a cherry, turn rosy—as do some of the joints. Most of the year it is not much of a looker, but in midsummer the bright yellow flowers add a gay note to the rock garden or some dry slope where the soil is thin and poor. To my tongue the fruits are most insipid. If for some reason you wish to encourage various cacti in a climate with "average" rainfall, resort to the raised-bed technique.

RELATED SPECIES: *O. polyacantha* is a spinier species often offered by western nurseries and also very hardy. The eastern sister has enough spines, incidentally, to warrent care when weeding in the area. The spines are small but difficult to remove from fingers.

PROPAGATION: By seed, but it is much easier to break off a joint in spring and prop it between some stones with just its lower edge in the soil until it roots.

Prickly-Pear (*Opuntia compressa*)

Pachistima (*Paxistima canbyi*)

FAMILY: Staff-tree (*Celastraceae*).

OTHER NICKNAMES: Mountain-lover, cliff-green.

HABITAT: Almost any well-drained soil with some humus; sun or partial shade.

DESCRIPTION: Very hardy dwarf evergreen, seldom as high as 12 in., with tiny hollylike leaves.

BLOOM PERIOD: Spring, but not important for its easily overlooked flowers.

OUTSTANDING FEATURES: Wonderful as an edging or a low evergreen note in foreground.

NATURAL RANGE: Mountains of Virginia and West Virginia, but can withstand temperatures as low as 20° below zero.

CULTURE: Avid rock gardeners know this useful little southerner, but it has been sadly overlooked by most growers and nurseries. Acres of pachysandra struggle over the American landscape where this would be a much better choice. In hot climates it might be best to give it some afternoon shade, but in the Philadelphia area it does fine in nearly full sun and soil that is more clay than the woodland duff the plant would be more apt to find in its native home. In shade plants will be less compact. Unless you have sharp eyes, you will never even notice the tiny spring flowers, nor are there any decorative fruits, but the graceful low mounds of green are a welcome note at any time of year and sport bronzy tints during the cold months. My plants are subjected to rather bad winter wind without damage. A mature individual plant covers perhaps a circle around 12 in. in diameter, but this is a genus that layers very easily. By covering the ends of a branch with a thin layer of dirt weighted down with a small stone, you can quickly encourage it either to cover a large round area or to make a straight edging. For the latter use, you may wish to shear it slightly in early spring, but it is inherently a mind-its-own-business kind of plant, so even that need be done only sparingly. The foliage is lovely in miniature arrangements, and cuttings can also be used in humid terrariums, where they often root.

RELATED SPECIES: *P. myrsinites* from the west is a taller species, growing up to 2 ft. high. Its branches are stiffer, so it is not as useful as a groundcover, nor has it proved as hardy in my garden.

PROPAGATION: By cuttings or stem layerings.

Pachistima (*Paxistima canbyi*)

Beard-Tongue (*Penstemon hirsutus*)

FAMILY: Figwort (*Scrophulariaceae*).
OTHER NICKNAMES: Hairy or eastern penstemon, pentstemon.
HABITAT: Thin, rocky, dry soil; sun, but will take partial shade.
DESCRIPTION: Airy clusters of lavender and white tubular flowers about an inch long on stems up to 18 in: high; basal foliage is evergreen (at least in eastern Pennsylvania), taking on a purply cast as weather grows colder.
BLOOM PERIOD: Spring into summer.
OUTSTANDING FEATURE: Thrives on dry, rocky banks.
NATURAL RANGE: Quebec to Ontario and Wisconsin; south to Virginia, Kentucky, and Tennessee.
CULTURE: There are more than 200 penstemons native to the western states, but they are not easy to cultivate in the east. Many are at best biennials; others cannot take prolonged periods of wet weather or the alternate freeze and thaw of eastern winters. This little easterner has no such temperamental habits if given a well-drained sunny spot. Winter wet is the greatest enemy. In a well-tended rock garden it may spread too quickly by seeding, but you can combat this by cutting off the flower heads before seed is set. There is a rarer pure white form which is delightful.
RECOMMENDED HYBRIDS: Several named cultivars of western penstemon have merit for the sunny garden: Garnet, Royal Beauty, Ruby King, Prairie Fire, Pink Beauty, Arroyo, Mesa. Most of them make plants 2 to 3 ft. high. Rose Elfe grows to 18 in., and Pat is an 8 in. pink form. Seed of the Viehmeyer hybrids is also available.
RELATED SPECIES: The tall smooth beard-tongue (*P. digitalis*) of the eastern states has heads of mostly white flowers on 3- to 4-ft. stems and is useful for the back of the border, where it blooms in midsummer. It is a rampant seeder, however, so cut back the plants after flowering. It, too, will take about half a day of shade successfully. *P. barbatus* (sometimes cataloged as *Chelone barbata*) and its variety *torreyi* are reds worth trying. *P. fruticosus* (lavender blue), *P. rupicola* (ruby red), *P. newberryi* (purple), and *P. davidsoni* (violet purple) are some tiny species suitable for rock gardens. All must have perfect drainage to survive.
PROPAGATION: By seed or transplanting of self-sown seedlings; by division in spring.

120

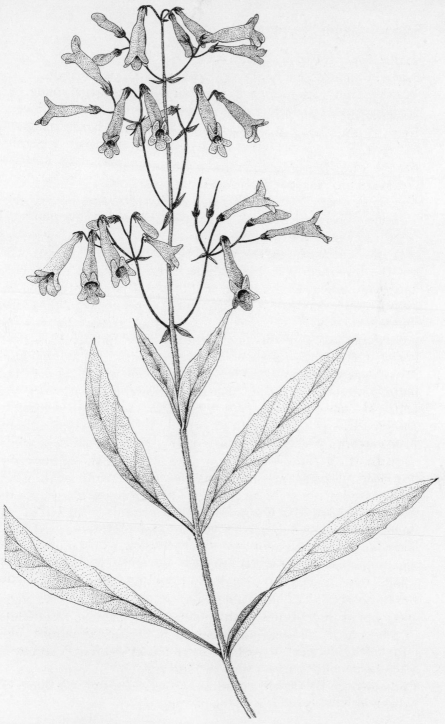

Beard-Tongue (*Penstemon hirsutus*)

Tall Phlox (*Phlox* Miss Lingard)

FAMILY: Phlox (*Polemoniaceae*).

OTHER NICKNAMES: Wild sweet William. Sometimes also designated botanically as *P. suffruticosa* or *glaberrima*.

HABITAT: Rich loam; nearly full sun.

DESCRIPTION: Dense clusters of fragrant white flowers on stems 2 to 3 ft. high.

BLOOM PERIOD: Early summer and often until fall.

OUTSTANDING FEATURE: The longest-flowering phlox.

NATURAL RANGE: This is a cultivated garden form and quite hardy.

CULTURE: There are about fifty species of phlox, all of American origin. I have never seen one I didn't love, but if I had to choose only one for the garden, this would be it. Catalogs list it variously, but the true form is a comfortable friend for life. It is ruggedly hardy and will grow nearly as well in partial shade as in full sun, asking only a rich loam and sufficient summer water. The mildew that affects foliage of other summer phlox seldom bothers the good green leaves of this one, although good air circulation and hosing early so the foliage is dry before sunset are always wise. Miss Lingard begins blooming in early June in my garden and literally keeps the process up all summer if old flowers are removed before seed sets. Every few years it pays to divide the plant in early spring to keep it thrifty.

RECOMMENDED SELECTIONS AND HYBRIDS: Reine du Jour, a white with a red eye, and Rosalinde, a fine pink, are two other early flowering phlox that give recurring bloom. The many forms of tall hardy summer phlox (often cataloged as *P. decussata*) are hybrids developed mostly by Europeans. They provide great trusses of flowers in pure white and every shade of pink, rose, red, and lavender, often with contrasting eye. They are far better for ordinary garden use than the true species, since they give greater color choice, larger flower heads, and are often taller.

RELATED SPECIES: *P. paniculata* and *P. maculata* are the main ancestors of the hybrids. Both exhibit color variation from white to magenta in the wild and do well in moister situations than afforded by the garden itself. Western nurseries offer *P. speciosa*, a 2 ft. bushy pink species found in Montana.

PROPAGATION: By division or stem cuttings in spring. Seedlings of hybrids will not breed true to the parents.

Tall Phlox (*Phlox* Miss Lingard)

Dwarf Phlox (*Phlox subulata*)

FAMILY: Phlox (*Polemoniaceae*).

OTHER NICKNAMES: Ground pink, moss pink, mountain pink.

HABITAT: Almost any well-drained soil; takes partial shade.

DESCRIPTION: Evergreen mats of needlelike foliage are nearly covered with flat flowers a few inches high in shades of white, pink, and lavender, sometimes with contrasting eye.

BLOOM PERIOD: Spring.

OUTSTANDING FEATURE: A fine groundcover for thin soil.

NATURAL RANGE: New York to Michigan; south to Maryland, North Carolina, and Tennessee.

CULTURE: In its various cultivated forms, this phlox is seen so much that few credit it with being a native flower. Some of the named forms now so popular were developed in England, but several of the best are merely selections from good wild plants. Although this is a common plant in cemeteries and rock gardens all over the country, it is not always used to its full potential. Pick the forms you plant with care, using perhaps a good white and one other shade as ribbons of color in the spring garden. Refrain from planting many different hues next to each other. A small start will spread into a great mat if there is sufficient sun and good drainage. The plants are very useful to provide a foliage foil for autumn crocus, which flowers without leaves of its own.

RECOMMENDED HYBRIDS AND SELECTIONS: There are many named cultivars, but do try Blue Hill and Scarlet Flame if they fit into your color scheme. *P. procumbens* is a hybrid with rosy purple blossoms.

RELATED SPECIES: *P. stolonifera* (creeping phlox) is a lovely thing for woodland spots that get spring sunshine. It wants a slightly more humusy soil somewhat on the acid side. Its bright pink flowers are borne on upright stems a few inches high in late spring; the leaves are round on stems creeping from evergreen basal rosettes. Blue Ridge is an outstanding color selection, and there is considerable variation in the wild. *P. ovata* (mountain phlox) is similar but taller with larger, later flowers, well worth a home in partial shade. *P. bifida* (cleft or sand phlox) has pale blue or white deeply cut petals and forms mounds about 10 in. high. It wants full sun and well-drained sandy soil.

PROPAGATION: Many by seed; also by division or stem cuttings in spring.

Dwarf Phlox (*Phlox subulata*, left; *Phlox stolonifera*, right)

White Obedient Plant *(Physostegia virginiana alba)*

FAMILY: Mint *(Labiatae)*.

OTHER NICKNAME: False-dragonhead. Also designated botanically as *Dracocephalum virginianum*.

HABITAT: Almost any soil with some humus; full sun.

DESCRIPTION: Spikes of white flowers somewhat resembling a snapdragon on stems 1 to 3 ft. tall; basal rosettes evergreen at least as far north as Pennsylvania.

BLOOM PERIOD: Summer.

OUTSTANDING FEATURE: A good white vertical for the summer garden.

NATURAL RANGE: Quebec to Minnesota; south to Tennessee and Louisiana.

CULTURE: Unlike its rose sister, this variety of physostegia is quite easy to control in the garden. Its height pretty much depends on the richness of the soil and the amount of moisture. The white does not demand the damp soil preferred by the type. Instead of spreading by creeping roots, the white variety puts out offset plants. Flower arrangers like physostegia both for its spiky effect and because the individual flowers can be pushed around the stem without harm to lie in any plane an arrangement calls for. Where the soil is too damp, the white physostegia may rot out, but it does not want too dry a summer either.

RECOMMENDED SELECTION: Summer Snow is a named white variety.

RELATED SPECIES: The more common *P. virginiana* may grow even taller than the white. Good rose-colored forms create a fine clump of color, but it is much harder to keep in bounds because of the creeping roots. Since the pink forms dote on damp situations, they are a good choice for a sunny wettish spot where other plants will not survive. One of the brightest selections is Summer Glow. Rosy Spire is late-blooming, and Vivid is a dwarf form seldom over 2 ft. high. There is also a pink-flowered variety with variegated white and green foliage.

PROPAGATION: White forms can be started from seed, but germination is often poor, so also try division in spring. From seed you can expect *P. virginiana* to give plants with flowers ranging from magenta to pale pink. Choose those that have the shade you prefer, destroy the rest, then propagate your favorites by division in spring.

White Obedient Plant (*Physostegia virginiana alba*)

Wild Petunia (*Ruellia strepens*)

FAMILY: Acanthus (*Acanthaceae*).
OTHER NICKNAME: Smooth ruellia.
HABITAT: Dry, sandy soil; nearly full sun.
DESCRIPTION: Blue violet flowers somewhat like a petunia on sprawly stems 1 to 3 ft. tall.
BLOOM PERIOD: Summer.
OUTSTANDING FEATURE: Good source of blue in the dry summer garden.
NATURAL RANGE: Pennsylvania to Kansas; south to Florida and Texas.
CULTURE: It is not easy to locate a source for any of the ruellias, but they provide such a pretty note in the summer garden that they are worth an extra search. Because of their more or less prostrate habit, they go best in the foreground. If the site is dry enough, they make a lovely sight on the sunny fringe of a woodland where there is little color after the big spring burst. They are also good choices for rock gardens and dry walls. Bloom can come any time after June and continues a long time. This species has the most northerly range of the genus and is worth trying if you can locate seed or plants. All must have perfect drainage.
RELATED SPECIES: *R. ciliosa* (hairy ruellia) is similar but perhaps more lavender and has a more southerly range. There are several other southern species. *R. humilis* is native to about the same area as *R. strepens* and reportedly hardy as far north as Illinois.
PROPAGATION: By seed; by division in spring.

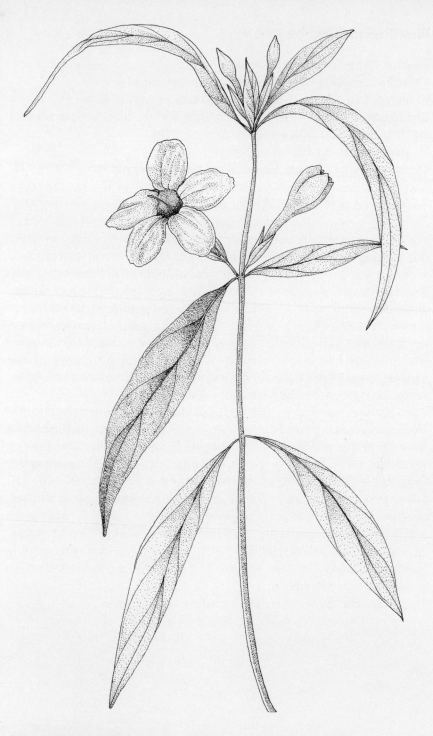

Wild Petunia (*Ruellia strepens*)

Fire-Pink (*Silene virginica*)

FAMILY: Pink (*Caryophyllaceae*).
OTHER NICKNAMES: Red catchfly, crimson campion.
HABITAT: Well-drained humusy soil; sun to partial shade.
DESCRIPTION: Sparse clusters of bright red stars an inch across on weak stems 1 to 2 ft. high.
BLOOM PERIOD: Spring into summer.
OUTSTANDING FEATURE: Vivid color over a long period.
NATURAL RANGE: Ontario to Minnesota; south to Georgia, Alabama, Arkansas, and Oklahoma.
CULTURE: Open woods and rocky hills are the natural habitats of this showy native. It does not want wetness but otherwise is fairly adaptable, being found in soil varying from neutral to acid and able to take differing hours of sunshine. In more northern climates it often grows in nearly full sun, but as it moves into warmer zones, fire-pink seems to like some filtered shade. Picking the old flowers off prolongs blooming. The sticky hairy stems on which small insects are often caught explain one nickname. The word *pink*, as applied to this family, refers not to the colors of the flowers but to the shape of the petals, which are often notched or laciniated as if trimmed with pinking shears.
RELATED SPECIES: *S. caroliniana* (*pensylvanica*) is called pink catchfly and is a beauty for the rock garden. It makes a low tuft barely 6 in. high and is studded in May with inch-wide pink flowers having petals wider than those of its red relative. It must have perfect drainage or the thick root rots in winter wet. The closely allied *S. wherryi* is even dwarfer. *S. hookeri* from the west coast is similar. *S. stellata* (starry campion) ranges between 2 and 3 ft. high with small white flowers during the summer; it should have part shade. *S. californica* (Indian pink), with its very pretty semidouble reddish flowers on 1-ft. stems, is from the mountains and so should be fairly hardy.
PROPAGATION: By seed; by stem cuttings after bloom.

Fire-Pink (*Silene virginica*)

Sweet Goldenrod (*Solidago odora*)

FAMILY: Daisy (*Compositae*).
OTHER NICKNAME: Anise-scented goldenrod.
HABITAT: Well-drained sandy soil, at least moderately acid; sun.
DESCRIPTION: Small clusters of yellow flowers on a slender wand 2 to 4 ft. high; narrow leaves emit anise smell when crushed.
BLOOM PERIOD: Summer.
OUTSTANDING FEATURES: Fragrance of leaves and small stature.
NATURAL RANGE: Nova Scotia to Florida and Texas.
CULTURE: There are more than 100 American goldenrods. So common are they that we seldom bring them into our gardens, but Europeans have selected and hybridized extensively. A few of these forms are for sale in this country and they are recommended for wider use in American gardens. I selected this species to feature partially at least because its dried leaves, when steeped in hot water, yield a pleasant tea. For garden use it does not spread as rampantly as some, and the slender flower spikes are easier to work into a border. Many other goldenrods have huge plumes or great flat-topped heads that require a lot of space. Most grow naturally in rather sterile soil. Brought into more fertile areas, they may become too tall or even blousy. *S. odora* is more particular than most in requiring acid soil. It takes a little shade.
RECOMMENDED HYBRIDS: Cloth of Gold had big spikes 20 in. high, flowers in August, and can last several months. Golden Mosa is lemon yellow and may grow to 3 ft. in late summer. Peter Pan, at 2 ft., is particularly neat with deep lemon plumes. Some others: Golden Thumb, 1 ft.; Crown of Rays, 2 ft.; Golden Wings, 6 ft.; Lemore, 30 in.
RELATED SPECIES: If you come across a wild goldenrod that appeals to you for one reason or other, you can usually bring it into your garden with a clear conscience. Goldenrod moves easily, seeds itself well, and—as far as I know—no species is the least endangered. Be careful, however, of those which spread by creeping roots; they are not easy to keep in bounds. You can tame some of the taller species by cutting them to about a foot in early summer to make shorter, bushier plants. Look for: *S. graminifolia*, a 3-footer, for damp spots; *S. canadensis*, with 5 ft. plumes; *S. juncea*, an early and very hardy species; *S. rigida*, which has 2- to 4-ft. flat heads. *S. bicolor* is a creamy biennial.
PROPAGATION: By seed; by division in spring.

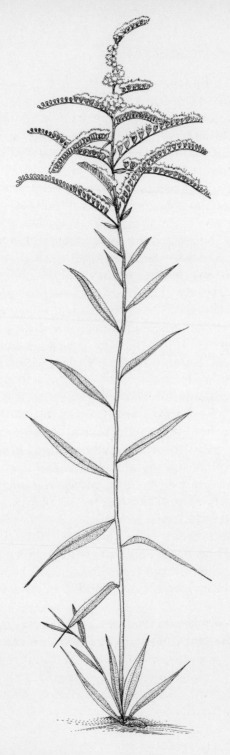

Sweet Goldenrod (*Solidago odora*)

Stokes-Aster (*Stokesia laevis*)

FAMILY: Daisy (*Compositae*).

OTHER NICKNAME: Cornflower aster. Sometimes botanically designated as *S. cyanea*.

HABITAT: Well-drained garden loam; nearly full sun.

DESCRIPTION: Fluffy blue to lavender flowers 2 to 5 in. across on well-branched stems 1 to 2 ft. high.

BLOOM PERIOD: Much of summer.

OUTSTANDING FEATURES: Both the long blooming period and the beauty of the flowers.

NATURAL RANGE: South Carolina to Florida and Louisiana.

CULTURE: Be patient with your stokesia until they have reached about three years old. At that point each will be literally covered with flowers on a bushy plant that needs nearly two square feet of room during flowering. By removing spent flowers you will gain sporadic bloom until September, but the thistly seedpods are also prized by arrangers of dried material. Although the natural range is southerly, I have found stokesia hardy without any protection in the Philadelphia area, and it is reported to withstand the winter as far north as Rochester, New York. Since it is such a good garden plant, try it wherever you live. In the north make sure it has good winter drainage and a warm, south-facing spot with some protection from the worst winter wind. It would even be worth lifting the plants to winter in a cold frame if your climate is too harsh, for it is truly a fine decorative. In my garden the basal foliage is evergreen without protection, and my plants bloom well even in a little filtered shade.

RECOMMENDED SELECTIONS: Blue Danube, Blue Star, and Blue Moon are named blue forms. Superba is more lavender, and Silver Moon is a good white. Bailey (see Bibliography) lists the varieties *lutea* (creamy yellow) and *rosea* (pink), but I have never seen either cataloged.

PROPAGATION: Easily grown from seed. There may be considerable variation in shades, but almost always color is on the blue side.

Stokes-Aster (*Stokesia laevis*)

Aaron's-Rod (*Thermopsis caroliniana*)

FAMILY: Pea (*Leguminosae*).
OTHER NICKNAMES: Bush-pea, golden-pea.
HABITAT: Almost any well-drained soil; full sun.
DESCRIPTION: Long terminal spires of good-sized yellow pea-flowers on stout stalks 3 to 5 ft. tall.
BLOOM PERIOD: Late spring.
OUTSTANDING FEATURE: Tall yellow note when accent plants are scarce.
NATURAL RANGE: North Carolina to Georgia.
CULTURE: A seedling thermopsis may not look like much, but in a few years it will increase into a clump nearly a foot across with many flowering stems. In rich soil it may grow so tall that it must have staking, but with sparser nourishment it can pretty much take care of itself. Always give it full sun or it will lean toward the light and then flop over. It belongs in the back of a garden or in sunny bays of shrubbery. The light green foliage stays fresh until frost. Thermopsis is often used as a substitute for perennial lupines because it is easier to grow, but of course lupines have a greater color range. The furry gray seedpods of the thermopsis resemble small string beans. (They make good ears for toy rabbits fashioned from small pine cones.) This native will survive in quite dry spots, especially if it has adequate moisture just before flowering begins. Northern gardeners should have no hesitation about trying it because it is native to the mountainous parts of the south rather than the warmer coastal plain. It has proven absolutely hardy in the Philadelphia area. Cut and dispose of the old stalks after frost as a precaution against stem borers, which sometimes attack a stalk.
RELATED SPECIES: *T. mollis* from drier sections of Virginia and Georgia is easier to work into a small garden because it seldom exceeds 3 ft. in height, but its flowers are not quite as showy. There are other species native to the west and to Alaska, most of them shorter than *T. caroliniana*. Unfortunately, seed of these lesser-known species is seldom available commercially.
PROPAGATION: By seed; by division in earliest spring.

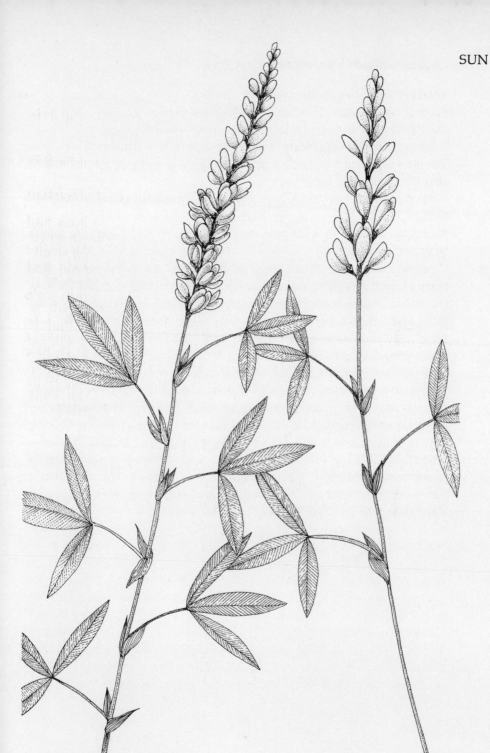

Aaron's-Rod (*Thermopsis caroliniana*)

Culver's-Root (*Veronicastrum virginicum*)

FAMILY: Snapdragon (*Scrophulariaceae*).
OTHER NICKNAMES: Culver's-physic, wild veronica.
HABITAT: Rich soil not lacking in moisture; mostly sun.
DESCRIPTION: Several long wands of tiny white flowers atop 3- to 5-ft. stems; whorls of foliage give neat appearance.
BLOOM PERIOD: Summer.
OUTSTANDING FEATURE: Gives a graceful fountain effect at back of the large garden or amid shrubbery.
NATURAL RANGE: Massachusetts and Vermont to Manitoba; south to Florida and Texas.
CULTURE: While Culver's-root is found in moist meadows and thickets in the wild, it does very well in the ordinary garden where the soil contains some humus. Although it will grow in half shade, it flowers much better in full sun. Because of its height and proclivity to spread into large clumps, this native is not easy to work into a small garden, but it is a knockout where it is in scale with its companions. If old flowers are faithfully removed, *V. virginicum* will bloom over a long stretch of the summer. Both in the garden and in bouquets, the long graceful flower plumes contrast delightfully with round blossoms of daisy form. During dry summers give extra water to keep it going. In time a clump may grow too large, but it is easy to remove extra creeping roots from the periphery. Culver's-root was named after an early American physician and was used as a cathartic and an emetic.
PROPAGATION: By seed; by division in spring.

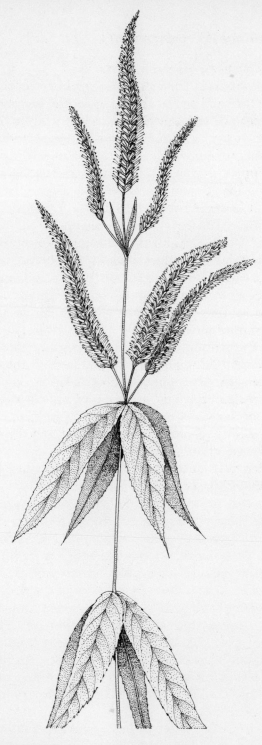

Culver's-Root (*Veronicastrum virginicum*)

Birdfoot Violet (*Viola pedata*)

FAMILY: Violet (*Violaceae*).

OTHER NICKNAMES: Crowfoot violet, pansy violet.

HABITAT: Well-drained, sandy, not fertile, very acid soil; full sun.

DESCRIPTION: Purple or lilac pansylike flowers as large as 1½ in. across above a low tuft of finely cut foliage.

BLOOM PERIOD: Spring, but may repeat during summer or fall.

OUTSTANDING FEATURES: The largest and probably showiest of the native violets.

NATURAL RANGE: Massachusetts to Ontario, Minnesota, and Kansas; south to Georgia and Texas.

CULTURE: Many of our native violets do well in large amounts of sunshine if other conditions are to their liking, but this star of the family definitely wants full sun. It also demands soil more acid than usually found in cultivated areas. Unless your property has such natural soil, prepare the bed carefully for this treasure, or its career in your garden will be fleeting. Make a slightly raised bed, holding the soil in with rocks if necessary. Mix coarse builder's sand and acid sphagnum peat into the soil. After planting, mulch well annually with pine needles. (All violets in sunny places benefit from a mulching.) Don't pick the birdfoot's flowers if you want increase, and it may seed itself. It produces no cleistogamous flowers (see *Viola pensylvanica*, page 230). This violet is a challenge—but so very beautiful.

RECOMMENDED SELECTIONS: Var. *bicolor* has blue and purple blossoms; *alba* is pure white.

RELATED SPECIES: *V. pedatifida* (the prairie or larkspur violet of the midwest) is nearly as splendid as the birdfoot and somewhat easier because it does not need so acid a soil. *V. halli* from the Oregon prairies also has finely cut leaves. It is yellow and violet. *V. sagittata* (arrow-leaf violet) likes sandy moist spots and will take a little shade. It has violet-purple flowers with a white center. *V. adunca* (sandland violet) from the west turns red purple as it matures. Among the whites *V. blanda* takes a lot of sun if in a good wet spot. The ubiquitous *V. sororia* (*papilionacea*) grows in both sun and shade if soil has some humus. A rampant spreader, it is best used as a groundcover under shrubs rather than in the garden itself. The whitish Confederate violet has the same reputation.

PROPAGATION: See under violets in shady plant section.

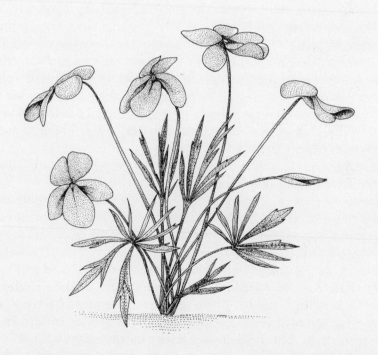

Birdfoot Violet (*Viola pedata*)

Adam's-Needle (*Yucca filamentosa*)

FAMILY: Lily (*Liliaceae*).

OTHER NICKNAMES: Spanish bayonet or dagger, beargrass, soapweed, heavenly candles. Sometimes botanically designated as *Y. smalliana.*

HABITAT: Dry, even arid, soil; full sun.

DESCRIPTION: Creamy white pendulous bells on tall leafless branched stalks 5 to 12 ft. high; foliage consists of tough, evergreen spears in a large imposing rosette 1 ft. tall. Threads often dangle from the points or margins of the leaves.

BLOOM PERIOD: Summer.

OUTSTANDING FEATURE: Gives bold effect in spots where soil is too dry or poor for anything else.

NATURAL RANGE: New Jersey to Florida and Mississippi.

CULTURE: I suppose if you were to plant a yucca in a swamp, you could kill it, but that's about the only way. Given the sunny, dry position it prefers, it will easily outlive the gardener who plants it. This species will even live in pure sand if given some watering until its great root gets deep enough to tap some moisture. This is not a plant for the small garden; the basal rosette can easily take a circle 2 ft. in diameter. In a large rock garden the foliage clumps make an interesting focal point even when the plant is not in flower. The large seedpods are useful in dried arrangements. This is another southerner that is hardy far into the north.

RECOMMENDED SELECTIONS: Bright Edge has variegated foliage. Var. *rosea* has flowers whose outside is tinged pink.

RELATED SPECIES: *Y. flaccida* from North Carolina and Alabama is harder to locate but easier to work into the garden, since its blossom stalks seldom exceed 6 ft. Its selection Ivory Towers is described as having outfacing or upright flowers, which would be showier. *Y. glauca* from the midwest is around 4 ft. high and surely hardy, since its range is from South Dakota to New Mexico. It also has a pink variety. There are numerous other species. Some of the far western ones are treelike, as is *Y. aloifolia* from the southern states, but these are not hardy in the north.

PROPAGATION: By seed; most frequently by root cuttings. Offsets from the main plant, with some root adhering, can also be cut off and propagated.

Adam's-Needle (*Yucca filamentosa*)

6
Plants for Shady Sites

In the hearts of many easterners of my generation a wild garden meant only one thing: a springtime woodland. The plants that made such spots magic in our childhood are the stars of this section. Happily for both us and the plants, the shadow of a single dogwood tree suffices to make a tiny microcosm of the forest. There is some shade on any property; the challenge is to make the most of it. Do note that some of these plants want only partial shade. However, they are in this section because they must have some protection from the sun; usually afternoon shade is preferred for them. Some plants described in either the section on moisture-loving plants or the section on sun-loving plants may also be ideal for shade or partial shade. Consult the Index to find the following:

Aconitum sp.
Arisaema sp.
Aster conspicuous
Aster cordifolius
Camassia sp.
Chamaelirium luteum
Delphinium sp.
Erythronium sp.
Eupatorium coelestinum
Gentiana sp.
Heliopsis helianthoides
Heuchera sp.
Lobelia cardinalis
Lobelia siphilitica

Paxistima sp.
Penstemon digitalis
Penstemon hirsutus
Phlox Miss Lingard
Phlox ovata
Phlox stolonifera
Saururus cernuus
Silene stellata
Silene virginica
Sisyrinchium sp.
Solidago odora
Thalictrum dioicum
Veronicastrum virginicum

Wood Leek (*Allium tricoccum*)

FAMILY: Lily (*Liliaceae*).
OTHER NICKNAMES: Ramps, ramsons, wild leek.
HABITAT: Rich, humusy soil; partial shade.
DESCRIPTION: Cluster of small white flowers on 12-in. stem appears after leaves wither. Leaves are about 2 in. wide and 6 to 10 in. long. They rest rather flatly on the soil and are quite decorative.
BLOOM PERIOD: Summer.
OUTSTANDING FEATURES: The wide, veined leaves are ornamental in spring.
NATURAL RANGE: New Brunswick and Quebec to Minnesota; south to Georgia, Tennessee, and Iowa.
CULTURE: With woodsy soil there is little trick to raising this American relative of the onion. Choose a spot under deciduous trees where there is early spring sunshine so that the leaves of the leek can pump nourishment back into the bulb during their brief growing period. Bruised, the leaves smell rankly of onion. If there is later shade, the flowers will last longer. Since there is no trace of foliage by then, an overplanting of something like *Asarum canadense* is a good technique. Its leaves do not become large until after the allium's are fading so cannot rob the latter of sun, and they serve nicely to set off the naked stems of the allium flowers. In the Appalachians, bulbs of this plant are avidly sought out in spring for food as soon as the leaves begin growth.
RELATED SPECIES: *A. cernuum* (summer wild onion) has a somewhat untidy cluster of nodding pink flowers on 1-ft. stalks and wants more sun than shade. The real star is *A. stellatum* from the midwest, which has small clusters of erect pink flowers atop 1-ft. stems in late summer and autumn. It, too, prefers nearly full sun, and both these alliums want well-drained, thin soil rather than woodland humus. Among many lesser-known western alliums, at least two are gardenworthy: *A. acuminatum* has loose purple clusters and *A. attenuifolium* dense pink or white clusters. Both are 1 ft. tall, bloom in late spring, and want nearly full sun. All alliums are lovely as cut flowers, and this is one way to keep them from spreading by seed, which sometimes can be too exuberant. The heads can also be dried for later arrangements.
PROPAGATION: By seed; by offsets gathered in early fall.

146

Wood Leek (*Allium tricoccum***)**

Rue-Anemone (*Anemonella thalictroides*)

FAMILY: Buttercup (*Ranunculaceae*).

HABITAT: Well-drained humusy soil on acid side; part shade.

DESCRIPTION: Several small white flowers with prominent yellow stamens, borne atop delicate leaves on wiry stems 4 to 8 in. tall.

BLOOM PERIOD: Spring.

OUTSTANDING FEATURE: A delightful plant to colonize the edge of the shady garden.

NATURAL RANGE: Maine to Minnesota; south to Florida, Alabama, Mississippi, and Oklahoma.

CULTURE: Altogether a charmer with no bad habits, this plant should be in every garden where there is some shade. As diminutive as it is, rue-anemone will fit in even the smallest niche. The flowers last a surprisingly long time, and the foliage is always decorative. When it does finally dry up in the summer, it does so very neatly. One of the further pleasures of having this plant in the garden is that the flowers and the whorl of dainty leaves dance with every slight breeze. Such motion makes a garden more interesting to look at and to be in as well. A few plants well self-sow into a thrifty patch in the right situation. Like dahlias, they grow from a cluster of tiny tubers. In my Pennsylvania garden the rue-anemone seems much happier if it has either filtered shade from the sun moving through high tree branches or is planted so that trees cast only afternoon shade. Perhaps farther north it can stand more sun, but it should always have shadow part of the day. Give the plants extra watering if late spring is very dry to encourage the foliage to grow as long as possible. Mice sometimes decimate a planting.

RECOMMENDED SELECTIONS: Pink, double, and semidouble forms exist, and flower size is variable, too. Schaaf's double pink as well as a double white are sometimes offered by dealers. These double flowers are long lasting small buttons completely filled with petals rather than having any stamens. While expensive, they are a beautiful investment for long-term garden enjoyment.

PROPAGATION: By seed; by division of tubers in summer after foliage dies, but this surgery is not always successful and I would forbear it myself.

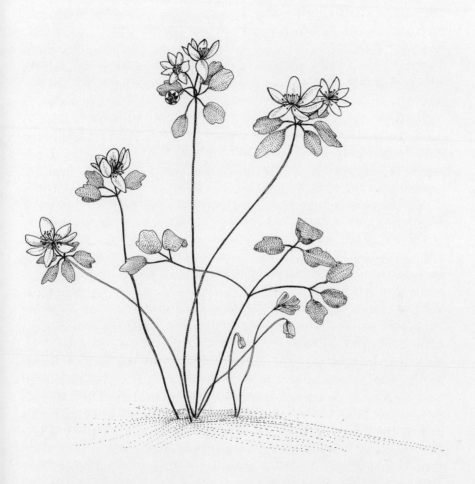

Rue-Anemone (*Anemonella thalictroides*)

Wild Columbine (*Aquilegia canadensis*)

FAMILY: Buttercup (*Ranunculaceae*).
OTHER NICKNAMES: Eastern columbine, American columbine.
HABITAT: Well-drained, not too rich soil; partial shade.
DESCRIPTION: Graceful flowers with long red spurs and yellow faces borne on stems 1 to 2 ft. above dainty compound foliage.
BLOOM PERIOD: Spring.
OUTSTANDING FEATURES: One of the easiest wildflowers to cultivate; a knockout en masse; foliage decorative all summer.
NATURAL RANGE: Quebec and Ontario to Wisconsin; south to Florida and Texas.
CULTURE: No garden should be without this undemanding but highly decorative American. Its slender flowers make the garden columbines look obese. I find it devilishly hard to photograph because the wiry flower stems are like tiny coils, and the blossoms bounce around in the slightest zephyr, but in the garden this is a plus, bringing motion. Hummingbirds seek out columbines for the nectar at the bottom of the spurs. Perhaps on the far northern fringes of its range, this aquilegia will take full sun, but I find that a partially shaded spot is much better, preferably one with morning sun or high filtered shade. This species flowers well even in a lot of shade but should get a bit of sun sometime during the day. In my garden the basal foliage is virtually evergreen, but it appears early everywhere and lasts until winter. This columbine revels in a rocky situation where its roots can get down into cooler soil. Your only precaution is to give it good drainage. In spots to its liking it will self-sow to make breathtaking sweeps of color.
RELATED SPECIES: Most of the long-spurred garden hybrids have at least one American parent. I have nothing against these, but the species have more charm and delicacy, and it is easier to get colonies of a single color. Several other native species are easy to find. *A. caerulea* (Rocky mountain columbine) has somewhat fat, long-spurred flowers in blue and white, wants acid soil and a cool exposure. *A. chrysantha* and *A. longissima* are both yellow with very long spurs and bloom later into summer. *A. saximontana*, a blue-and-yellow dwarf from Utah, wants a limy soil. *A. jonesi* is a tiny, difficult, acid-loving dwarf beloved by rock gardeners.
PROPAGATION: By seed. Transplant while still small.

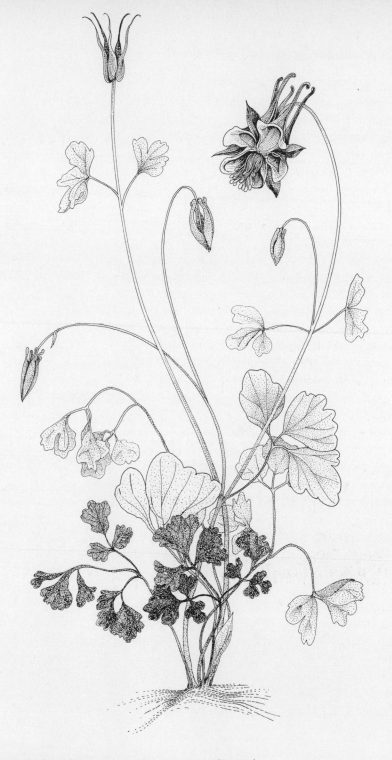

Wild Columbine (*Aquilegia canadensis*)

Goat's-Beard (*Aruncus dioicus*)

FAMILY: Rose (*Rosacea*).
OTHER NICKNAME: Wild spirea.
HABITAT: Rich humusy soil; partial shade.
DESCRIPTION: Many showy plumes of tiny white flowers on plants growing as high as 6 ft.; compound foliage.
BLOOM PERIOD: Summer.
OUTSTANDING FEATURES: Exuberant flowering and growth; almost bushlike.
NATURAL RANGE: New York to Kentucky; south to Georgia and Alabama.
CULTURE: Although not suited to the small garden, the goat's-beard deserves more attention from gardeners with large shady areas at their disposal. It brings color to such spots later in the growing season after most of the usual spring show is over in a conspicuous kind of display with the large feathery sprays of the blossoms held well above the foliage. Male and female flowers grow on separate plants, but there is little difference between them. This plant does quite well in moist bottomland and should not lack for summer water. It is often found in ravines in the wild. Because it wants partial shade rather than deep shadow, it is a good choice for sites under groups of high trees where the light is filtered and the soil not too dry. As might be guessed from the foliage and flowers, it is closely related to both astilbe and spirea, and sometimes it may be listed under either classification in catalogs. It often self-sows and is hardy farther north than its natural range.
RELATED SPECIES: *A. sylvester* is quite similar and found in our western states as well as Europe.
PROPAGATION: By seed; by division in spring.

Goat's-Beard (*Aruncus dioicus*)

Wild Ginger (*Asarum shuttleworthi*)

FAMILY: Birthwort (*Aristolochiaceae*).

OTHER NICKNAMES: Heartleaf, large-flowered hexastylis. Sometimes designated botanically as *A. grandiflorum*.

HABITAT: Rich, humusy soil on acid side; full shade.

DESCRIPTION: Heart-shaped evergreen foliage that is often oddly mottled and only a few inches high. The flower is a curious maroon "bottle" hidden under the leaves.

BLOOM PERIOD: Spring.

OUTSTANDING FEATURES: A good slow-growing evergreen groundcover for deep shade.

NATURAL RANGE: Virginia and West Virginia; south to Georgia and Alabama.

CULTURE: This southern species is hardy into the north so if you find it will winter in your garden, it is highly recommended because its foliage is evergreen. Often in northern gardens there will be a purple tinge to the winter leaves. All the wild gingers prosper in complete shade, and all do best with plenty of humus in the soil. All also make wonderful groundcovers under shrubs. The odd flowers lie right on the ground and are seldom noticed. Country children often term them "little brown jugs." Your only concern should be that the gingers have some extra water in periods of drought, particularly if they are competing with shrub or tree roots. The rootstocks and often the leaves have a ginger odor and a hot spicy taste.

RELATED SPECIES: *A. virginicum* has thicker, slightly smaller leaves. *A. arifolium* has triangular-shaped leaves and probably is not as hardy. *A. caudatum*, the western wild ginger, has the largest leaves of all. The lobes of its flowers are stretched out into tail-like appendages 2 in. long. *A. canadense* is much the hardiest species, with a natural range that extends well into Canada. Unfortunately, its heart-shaped leaves are not evergreen, but it makes a good, rather quick-spreading groundcover in shady places. It also tolerates soil that is drier and on the neutral side. I even have some increasing nicely in a spot that is so dry the ginger leaves wilt in summer if there is no rain.

PROPAGATION: By division in spring. Root cuttings take easily in damp peat moss.

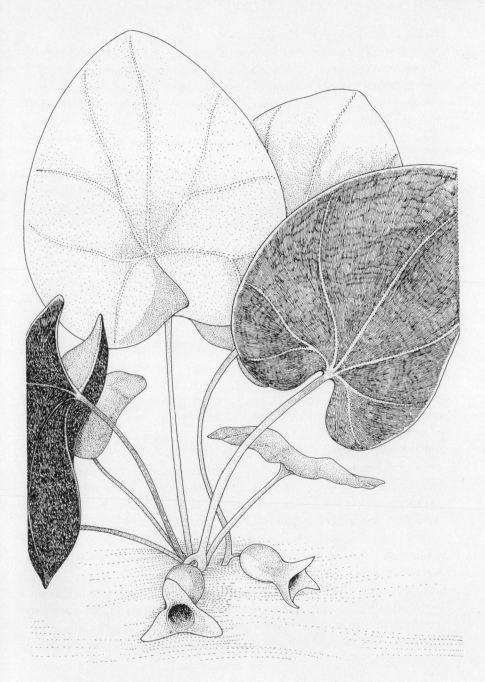

Wild Ginger (*Asarum shuttleworthi*)

Striped Pipsissawa (*Chimaphila maculata*)

FAMILY: Wintergreen (*Pyrolaceae*).

OTHER NICKNAME: Spotted wintergreen.

HABITAT: Well-drained, very acid, humusy soil; nearly full shade.

DESCRIPTION: Leathery dark evergreen leaves with quite striking white markings. The several terminal nodding white or pinkish flowers borne a few inches high are fragrant.

BLOOM PERIOD: Summer.

OUTSTANDING FEATURES: An interesting underplanting for beech, oak, and pine trees, but there is never enough foliage to qualify *C. maculata* as a groundcover. Lovely in terrariums.

NATURAL RANGE: New Hampshire to Ontario, Michigan and Illinois; south to Georgia and Tennessee.

CULTURE: Nothing could be more charming than some of these plants enlivening the landscape under mature beech trees, where almost nothing else gets enough light to prosper. The pipsissawas send up shoots along a long underground root, so that it appears as if there were many plants, but all are connected though separated by open space. Unless the soil is very acid, they simply do not take to ordinary shady gardens. However, sometimes they will last a few seasons before dying out. By using very acid leafmold you can prepare a proper site, but because of the wandering roots a small enclosed special area does not work too well. For most of us it is better to enjoy them as an accent plant in a winter terrarium and let it go at that, at least until we build up a naturally acid spot under a pine or an oak. The waxy flowers can be a real delight in the shade of a hot summer's day. Bloom seems to be best where the plants get just a bit of filtered sunshine during the day.

RELATED SPECIES: *C. umbellata* (prince's-pine) has unmottled lighter green whorls of foliage on somewhat longer stems, but otherwise has the same habits and demands. *C. menziesi* is a western form.

PROPAGATION: By seed in acid medium but difficult. Cuttings with some root sometimes take in an acid-soil terrarium but save as much root runner as possible, even rolling it up into a ball before planting, and keep in terrarium at least a year before transplanting in early spring.

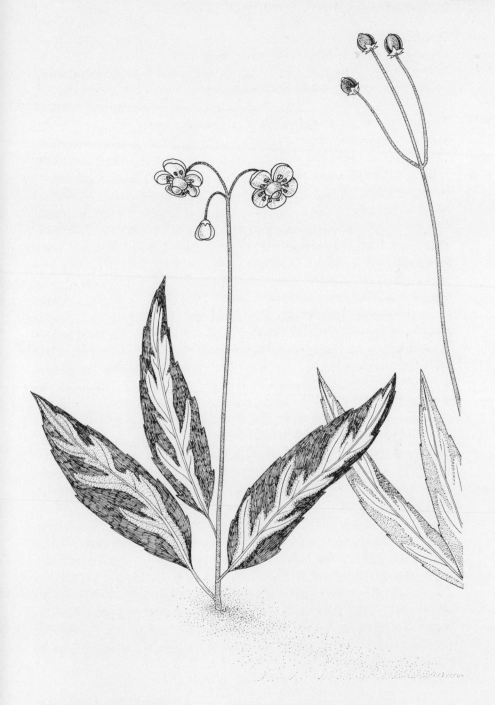

Striped Pipsissawa (*Chimaphila maculata*)

Golden-Star (*Chrysogonum virginianum*)

FAMILY: Daisy (*Compositae*).

HABITAT: Well-drained, humusy soil; partial shade.

DESCRIPTION: Yellow daisies as much as 2 in. across above hairy leaves on creeping stems that elongate as the season progresses to make a mound nearly 1 ft. high. Its foliage is evergreen, even in bitter cold, although not particularly attractive.

BLOOM PERIOD: Spring into summer.

OUTSTANDING FEATURE: Where hardy, a superb long-blossoming plant for the half-shady garden.

NATURAL RANGE: Pennsylvania and West Virginia; south to Florida and Louisiana.

CULTURE: Northern gardeners are advised to locate this little daisy in a protected spot, even in full sun. They should make sure, however, that it does not dry out during the summer. In the area of its natural range, grow it in partial shade without any protection whatever. When the plants first flower, they are only a few inches high, but the last blooms of the season may be on stems anywhere from 4 to 12 in. high. In the right location golden-star may have a very long blooming season, especially if the old heads are carefully removed to prevent seed formation. When preparing soil for planting, incorporate peat moss and some pebbles, too, if drainage is the least bit questionable. Although good drainage is essential, I must admit that I have one patch on a slight slope that must be artificially watered much of the summer to assure continued bloom. All these precautions are to keep the plants flowering as long as possible, but admittedly the spring show is always the most floriferous. Afternoon shade or filtered shade are the better choices of site in most of its range, and the bright yellow of its petals is a real surprise in the shade. You may not find it easy to locate starting plants, although more dealers are beginning to appreciate golden-star's worth. Southern wildflower suppliers are your best bets, but at least one New Jersey dealer has carried it. The northern-grown plants might be hardier. Golden-star is so excellent a plant it is even worth wintering plants over in a cold frame if necessary. Once transplanted and strong, the plants will self-sow as well as spread from stolons into good-sized patches. It is ideal for rock gardens.

PROPAGATION: By seed; by division in spring.

Golden-Star (*Chrysogonum virginianum*)

Fairy-Candle (*Cimicifuga americana*)

FAMILY: Buttercup (*Ranunculaceae*).
OTHER NICKNAMES: Bugbane, snakeroot, summer cohosh.
HABITAT: Rich, humusy soil; partial shade.
DESCRIPTION: Long slender wands of tiny white flowers on leafy stalks 2 to 4 ft. tall; foliage good as accent.
BLOOM PERIOD: Late summer.
OUTSTANDING FEATURE: Late-season focal point for shady garden.
NATURAL RANGE: Pennsylvania and West Virginia; south to Georgia and Tennessee.
CULTURE: Given a choice, I would plant this species rather than the more common one described below. For one thing, its plants do not grow as tall, a factor to consider in the smaller garden. For another, they bloom later in the year when there is so little color in the woodland. Finally, they do not share the somewhat fetid odor of their taller sister. In moister soil it is possible to grow the cimicifugas in nearly full sun, but their ability to take shade makes them more valuable for shady sites, since there are lots of blossoms in the sunny garden during August and September. However, a touch of sun during the day means better plants. Both species want a fertile soil that is on the acid side, and the addition of a rich mulch such as compost in spring is beneficial.
RELATED SPECIES: Flowers of *C. racemosa* (black cohosh or snakeroot) are similar but have a rank odor—the Latin generic name translates as bugbane. With a more northerly range, this species is probably much hardier, however. It blooms during the early summer. Clumps of plants may be 3 to 8 ft. tall, depending on soil fertility and available moisture. Both species are showy perennials that may be left in place for many years.
PROPAGATION: By seed sown in fall, but this form of propagation is not easy; also by division of roots in spring.

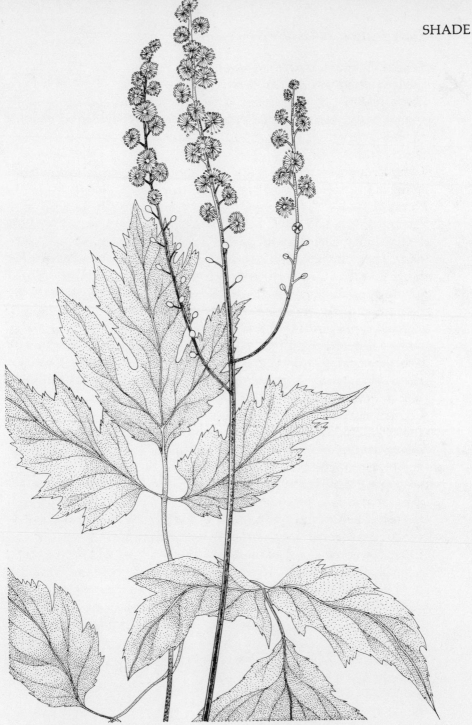

Fairy-Candle (*Cimicifuga americana*)

Spring-Beauty (*Claytonia virginica*)

FAMILY: Purslane (*Portulacaceae*).
HABITAT: Rich, moist loam; partial shade.
DESCRIPTION: Loose clusters of small, fragrant, white to pink flowers, with deep pink veining, growing a few inches above the narrow leaves.
BLOOM PERIOD: Spring.
OUTSTANDING FEATURES: A dainty charmer for early spring carpeting in low spots in garden or under trees.
NATURAL RANGE: Quebec to Ontario; south to Georgia and Texas.
CULTURE: Although this native grows in quantity in the wild despite bulldozers, buy some tubers rather than trying to collect them. They are difficult to locate, being sometimes quite deep, and the plant stems are so brittle you cannot help but break them. Deprived of nourishment from the foliage, the tuber easily dies. In the garden, plant them only 3 to 4 in. deep. They will soon self-sow into a fine drift. Claytonias are quite adaptable to a variety of garden soils and situations, but some humus in the soil is essential. They like spring moisture, and filtered shade is best. Since the leaves grow most of the winter, the plants can make themselves right at home under deciduous trees where there is winter sun. The succulent leaves disappear not long after flowering. There is much color variation in the wild, and semidouble forms are not unusual. To my knowledge there has not yet been any formal selection. Bloom lasts a long time, and new flowers are often still coming at the top of the stem while seeds are forming at the bottom. In quantity the fragrance is notable, but do not pick this wildflower because it wilts almost at once. The Indians ate the tubers, which are reputed to taste like potatoes when cooked.
RELATED SPECIES: *C. caroliniana* has wider leaves and a somewhat more northerly range. There is evidence it hybridizes with the narrow-leaved species when the two are planted closely together. *C. lanceolata* is a very hardy western broad-leaved species. *C. megarrhiza* is from the Rockies; it has a thick underground root and blooms very early.
PROPAGATION: By seed; by division of tubers when dormant.

Spring-Beauty (*Claytonia virginica*)

Bead-Lily (*Clintonia umbellata*)

FAMILY: Lily (*Liliaceae*).

OTHER NICKNAMES: White or speckled clintonia.

HABITAT: Rich, humusy soil that is on the acid side; full shade.

DESCRIPTION: Erect clusters of fragrant small white flowers with bronze dots on stalks up to 8 in. high; interesting basal rosette of foliage; black fruits.

BLOOM PERIOD: Late spring.

OUTSTANDING FEATURE: Leaves stay decorative all summer.

NATURAL RANGE: New York to Ohio; south in the mountains to Georgia and Tennessee.

CULTURE: Because it requires only moderately acid soil, this is the easier of the easterners to work into the garden. Using plenty of sphagnum peat humus for the initial planting will help. Mulch well to keep the site moist and cool during the summer. A colony is lovely in bloom but also a boon afterward, as the upright leaves make a nice minor accent in the woodland. Like its more northerly species, this is a creeper; new buds are formed on the ends of runners that fork from the old underground root. The latter dies afterward, hence a colony is annually on the move. For that reason, space plants quite far apart.

RELATED SPECIES: *C. borealis* (bluebead) has fewer pendant yellow flowers but the same good foliage and blue berries. Its natural range extends well into Canada; its southernmost habitats are definitely limited by heat. To prosper, *C. borealis* must have a cool, moist, shaded spot, and the soil must be strongly acid. These conditions are not always easy to meet. Since the flowers of the white species are more attractive, most gardeners are advised to try it first. *C. andrewsiana* of California's redwood country has umbels of small reddish purple flowers on stalks up to 18 in. high. The queen's-cup (*C. uniflora*) is a real beauty with solitary white bells an inch or so wide just above foliage which resembles that of lily-of-the-valley. Plants are only about 6 in. tall, and a colony is very pretty in bloom. Both westerners want cool, woodland habitats.

PROPAGATION: By seed, but it takes many years before flowering. Early spring or fall division of new roots must be done carefully. Reset with bud tips just under the soil and runners about an inch deep.

Bead-Lily (*Clintonia umbellata*)

Bunchberry (*Cornus canadensis*)

FAMILY: Dogwood (*Cornaceae*).

OTHER NICKNAMES: Dwarf cornel, creeping dogwood.

HABITAT: Cool, moist, very acid soil; full shade.

DESCRIPTION: Creamy white bracts just like a miniature dogwood flower above a whorl of oval leaves a few inches high.

BLOOM PERIOD: Late spring.

NATURAL RANGE: Greenland and Labrador to Alaska; south to Maryland, the Great Lakes, South Dakota, New Mexico, and California.

CULTURE: Although its stated range makes it seem practically ubiquitous, in southern parts of its natural haunts the bunchberry is found only in the mountains, where the summers are cool. In southeastern Pennsylvania, where it is hot much of the summer, these plants must be sited very carefully, and even then they do not grow luxuriously. Farther north, bunchberry is often treated as a groundcover in shady spots, where it spreads by means of underground runners into fine colonies, but we cannot expect such growth in the Philadelphia area. Where summers are hot, you must look for a cool place where the humus-rich soil is moist and very acid, and you must mulch frequently with pine needles. These pretty plants are tiny relatives of the dogwood tree, and the leaves color similarly in the fall before they drop. The cluster of red berries formed in the fall is much like those sported on the eastern dogwood tree, hence the popular name. Those who have a moist, very acid spot where summer heat never penetrates can create a unique garden with bunchberry, painted trillium, bluebeads, and other plants that demand the same conditions. I am told the bunchberry does very well in the cool climate of the northwestern states, too, but it is especially beloved in New England and Canada. Perhaps in those northern latitudes it may take a bit of morning sun, but farther south it must have complete shade. Mine are in low ground under a white pine tree where the sun never enters, the soil stays moist, and fallen pine needles keep the upper soil acid.

PROPAGATION: Separate seed from berries and plant in the fall in a very acid medium outdoors. Runners may root in a terrarium or a damp sand-and-peat mixture in a cold frame. Large sods can also be transplanted but must be watered faithfully and mulched until the plants make themselves at home in the new site.

Bunchberry (*Cornus canadensis*)

Yellow Lady-Slipper (*Cypripedium calceolus* var. *pubescens*)

FAMILY: Orchid (*Orchidaceae*).

OTHER NICKNAMES: Yellow slipper or moccasin orchid, whip-poor-will shoe.

HABITAT: Well-drained, humusy soil; full shade but good light.

DESCRIPTION: One or two odd flowers with inflated yellow sacs, the sepals and twisted side petals brown, atop a stalk 1 to 2 ft. high; prominently veined leaves up to 6 in. long.

BLOOM PERIOD: Spring, but foliage decorative later.

OUTSTANDING FEATURE: The easiest native orchid to cultivate.

NATURAL RANGE: Nova Scotia and Maine to Minnesota; south to North Carolina, Georgia, and Missouri.

CULTURE: Everyone wants native orchids, but few gardens can supply the conditions most of them want. This one, however, will make itself at home in a variety of soils from neutral to slightly acid, in dampish as well as fairly dry spots, and in many different climates. Since it is quite as pretty as any of its picky sisters, you need shed no tears if it is the only one you have. The root should be planted about an inch deep. Add plenty of humus when planting and mulch with leafmold or compost every spring. The plants should have light shade all day even in northern gardens. If summer is very dry, they benefit from a good soaking now and then. You want the foliage to luxuriate as long as possible. Some gardeners suggest a few cooling rocks for the roots to crawl under, but this may encourage slugs, which are a real menace to these plants. If you use rocks, put some slug bait under them in summer. If happy, this lady-slipper will slowly increase into nice clumps and might even self-sow.

RELATED SPECIES: Var. *parviflorum* is a fragrant smaller but quite similar yellow orchid native to more northern areas. Most authorities suggest you choose which to grow by where you live. Both are found in Pennsylvania, but this one must have a damper, cooler site. Many catalogs do not differentiate, but if you buy stock from a northern dealer you are most likely to get *parviflorum*; while southern houses handle *pubescens*. *C. reginae* (showy lady-slipper) is pink and white, wants moist, cool, woodsy soil and perhaps is the next least difficult. Not recommended for gardens: *C. acaule* (pink moccasin), which needs strongly acid soil; *C. arietinum* (ram's head), which wants a cool acid bog; and *C. candidum*, requiring a cool, limy, damp site.

PROPAGATION: Not easy from seed; by division in spring.

Yellow Lady-Slipper *(Cypripedium calceolus* var. *pubescens)*

Fringed Bleeding-Heart (*Dicentra eximia*)

FAMILY: Fumitory (*Fumariaceae*).

OTHER NICKNAMES: Turkey-corn, staggerweed, plumy or wild bleeding-heart.

HABITAT: Moist, humusy soil on acid side; half shade.

DESCRIPTION: Clusters of pink to rose flowers; bluish fernlike foliage 6 to 18 in. tall in fountainlike growth.

BLOOM PERIOD: Spring to hard frost.

OUTSTANDING FEATURES: Long bloom period, graceful daintiness.

NATURAL RANGE: New York to Pennsylvania and West Virginia; south to Georgia and Tennessee.

CULTURE: If you have room for but one plant in a shady garden, this eastern species (or one of the hybrids recommended below) should be your choice. Few perennials from any part of the world can match their long flowering season. Even when not in flower the foliage is always attractive. Where summers are hot, wild bleeding-heart may sulk and send out few blossoms until the days grow cooler again, but you can encourage ever-blooming by making sure it never lacks for moisture. Use plenty of peat moss when planting and mulch with pine bark for best results. Position is all-important. This plant must have some shade, particularly where midsummer is blazing, but it must also have adequate light. I find the eastern fringes of deciduous trees best. Here the morning sun can reach in, but the trees cast cooling shadow as the day warms up. *D. eximia* may seed itself but is never weedy, and it is hard to see how any garden could have too much of it.

RECOMMENDED HYBRIDS AND SELECTIONS: There are some fine cultivars: Bountiful, Luxuriant, Summer Beauty, Valentine, and Zestful are good rose forms; Sweetheart is pure white. All have the same long blooming period as *D. eximia* if conditions are to their liking.

RELATED SPECIES: *D. formosa* and *D. oregana* are overblooming western species somewhat shorter than *D. eximia*. The former is usually rose, the latter white and rose; both spread by creeping stolons. The eastern *D. cucullaria* (Dutchman's-breeches) and *D. canadensis* (squirrel-corn) have mostly white blooms but go dormant after spring, hence are not nearly as useful.

PROPAGATION: By seed; by division in early spring. Some species have tiny bulblets.

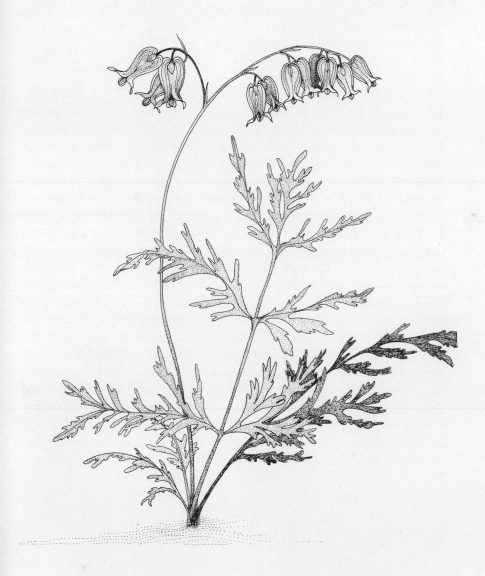

Fringed Bleeding-Heart (*Dicentra eximia*)

Fairybells (*Disporum lanuginosum*)

FAMILY: Lily (*Liliaceae*).
OTHER NICKNAMES: Yellow mandarin, hairy disporum.
HABITAT: Rich, humusy soil; shade.
DESCRIPTION: One or two small greenish white bells at the tips of branched stems 1 to 2 ft. tall; red berries.
BLOOM PERIOD: Late spring.
OUTSTANDING FEATURE: Veined leaves make interesting accent.
NATURAL RANGE: New York to Ontario; south to Georgia, Alabama, and Tennessee.
CULTURE: While hardly a flamboyant sort of plant, fairybells lends a quiet note of cheer to the shady garden late in the spring when most other plants are already through flowering. The red berries bring additional color later. It flourishes equally well in either neutral or somewhat acid soil as long as there is sufficient humus content. While disporum rather favors slopes, it must never be allowed to dry out too much. A few rocks over the roots help keep things cool. All members of this genus tend to hide their bells beneath the foliage, but every garden needs a few shyer members, if only to contrast with the exhibitionists.
RELATED SPECIES: *D. smithi* from the Pacific northwest is perhaps the showiest member of the family. Its whitish flowers can be as long as an inch atop 3-ft. stems; berries are yellow. *D. oreganum* (gold-drops) has white bells and yellow berries and probably is a bit hardier. The eastern *D. maculatum* (nodding mandarin or spotted disporum) has a somewhat more southerly range than its hairy sister, but it is still hardy at least into most northern states. Its somewhat larger flowers come a few weeks earlier and are yellow, spotted with dark purple, but they are hidden more under the leaves. All want the same woodsy conditions.
PROPAGATION: Depulp seeds and sow at once in fall; by division of rootstock in spring or fall when dormant.

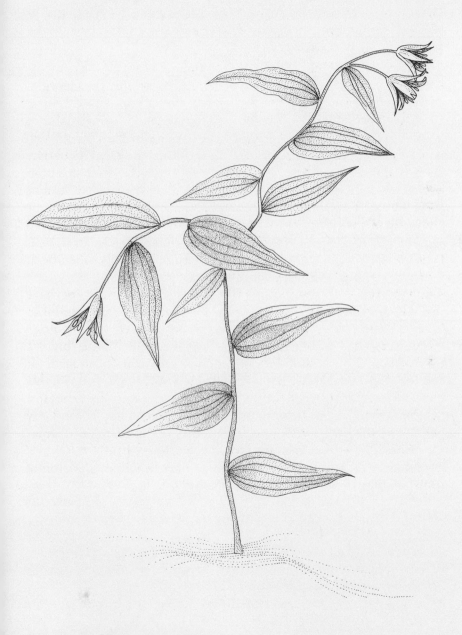

Fairybells (*Disporum lanuginosum*)

Shooting-Star (*Dodecatheon meadia*)

FAMILY: Primrose (*Primulaceae*).

OTHER NICKNAMES: American cowslip, prairie-pointers.

HABITAT: Neutral, humusy, well-drained soil; partial shade.

DESCRIPTION: Umbels of pink or white flowers with the petals so reflexed they resemble tiny rockets appear on a stem about 12 in. above a basal leaf rosette.

BLOOM PERIOD: Late spring.

OUTSTANDING FEATURE: A showy jewel for the discriminating.

NATURAL RANGE: Pennsylvania to Manitoba; south on uplands to Georgia, Louisiana, and Texas.

CULTURE: All the dodecatheons are North American, and a prettier gift to the gardens of the world is hard to imagine. Many authorities suggest that this species wants acid soil, but in my garden, where soil is on the acid side, I have been able to keep this plant more successfully by mulching it with marble chips, which definitely leach lime. Such a technique also serves to mark the site of the shooting-star, a good practice because the foliage disappears completely not too long after flowering; and it would be heart-breaking to dig inadvertantly into a planting. Dodecatheon likes filtered shade best, but if you cannot give it that, locate plants so they get afternoon shade. Drainage must be good, but the plants should not dry out either. If spring is very dry, I give mine extra water while the foliage is growing. All members of this family are especially good for rock gardens, and it may be that their roots like the cool of a protective rock. The marble chips would provide that, too.

RECOMMENDED SELECTION: Some dealers offer the white form separately as var. *albidum*.

RELATED SPECIES: *D. amethystinum* (jewel shooting-star) is smaller, has deep purple-pink flowers and blooms earlier. It definitely wants a cool situation, and I have found it more difficult to cultivate. The large shooting-star (*D. jeffreyi*) from the west has deep red-purple flowers on stems up to 18 in. tall, leaves to 12 in. long, and wants shade, humus, and adequate moisture. Any dodecatheon you can locate is worth garden space. Western dealers are most apt to have others. Most are on the pink or rose side, but many have white forms.

PROPAGATION: By seed, but mulch the bed well the first winter; by division in spring; by root cuttings.

Shooting-Star (*Dodecatheon meadia*)

Trailing Arbutus (*Epigaea repens*)

FAMILY: Heath (*Ericaceae*).
OTHER NICKNAMES: Mayflower, ground-laurel.
HABITAT: Light, porous soil, strongly acid; partial shade.
DESCRIPTION: A prostrate mat of evergreen foliage; small fragrant white to pink flowers in clusters at ends of stems.
BLOOM PERIOD: Early spring.
OUTSTANDING FEATURE: Where it will grow, a lovely groundcover.
NATURAL RANGE: Labrador to Saskatchewan; south to Florida and Mississippi.
CULTURE: Many eastern wildflower enthusiasts gauge success by whether they have trailing arbutus in the garden; but don't even try this unless you know your soil is very acid. If the soil is wrong, even the healthiest plants sicken and die out. The fringe of a pine tree where needle drop has had many years to build up an acid reaction in the soil is one good location. It may also do well as an underplanting for blueberries or acid-loving azaleas. Always mulch small plants well with pine needles or oak leaves. While arbutus wants a well-drained site, it also needs extra moisture where summers are hot or dry. And to bloom well there must be some hours of sunshine. What bothers conservationists is that gardeners keep buying this plant without any real idea of how difficult it is unless its wants are strictly satisfied. And many dealers obtain collected stock from an already depleted wild supply instead of troubling to raise their own. The most well-meaning attempt to cultivate arbutus fails if the surrounding soil is not very acid. Test the soil if you're not sure; it must have a pH of 4.5 for the arbutus to prosper. Some dealers offer sods in spring. Plant them undivided with lots of sphagnum moss added to the surrounding soil, mulch well, and make sure they never dry out that first year.
PROPAGATION: Difficult from seed. With established plants, stem layering works quite well. Cuttings taken in late summer and kept in a terrarium or cold frame also root in a year or so, but an extra year of nursing in a protected spot where the small plants can be watched and watered as needed is also a good precaution.

Trailing Arbutus (*Epigaea repens*)

White Snakeroot (*Eupatorium rugosum*)

FAMILY: Daisy (*Compositae*).

OTHER NICKNAMES: American ageratum, throughwort. Also variously designated botanically as *E. fraseri, E. urticaefolium,* or *E. ageratoides.*

HABITAT: Almost any well-drained soil; partial shade.

DESCRIPTION: Dense, flat-topped clusters of fluffy white flowers on stems 1 to 4 ft. tall.

BLOOM PERIOD: Fall.

OUTSTANDING FEATURE: A lovely white note for the shady garden in autumn.

NATURAL RANGE: Gaspe to Saskatchewan; south to Louisiana and Texas.

CULTURE: Unlike most of its sisters, this eupatorium prefers dryish sites and at least partial shade. Since it will bloom well under rather dense shade, it is a fine choice for the woodland garden where there is little other fall color except green. Because it needs so little moisture, it will also survive very close to tree trunks where other plants cannot compete. I particularly like it under dogwoods, where its good green leaves and snowy flowers contrast beautifully with the reddish maroon of the fall dogwood foliage. During summer drought the white snakeroot plants will droop dreadfully if planted in soil deficient in humus, and sometimes it is necessary to give them a soaking. They snap right back. Bloom is best with a touch of sun sometime during the day. With competition from tree roots, the plants seldom grow much higher than 2 ft. White snakeroot makes a dainty cut flower to use as a filler with other blooms like marigolds and zinnias, which are somewhat stiff looking. Cutting flowers is one way to combat the proclivity to self-sow. Another is to remove the spent flowers before they can form seed. This latter act not only lessens the weeding you might have to do the next year, but it will be appreciated by dairy farmers in your area, since the seeds are easily wind blown. Cows that eat this plant give poisonous milk that can cause fatal human illness.

RELATED SPECIES: Several other eupatoriums are described in the sunny plant section.

PROPAGATION: By seed; by division in spring.

White Snakeroot (*Eupatorium rugosum*)

Wandflower (*Galax rotundifolia*)

FAMILY: Diapensia (Diapensiaceae).

OTHER NICKNAME: Beetleweed. Sometimes given the botanical name *G. aphylla*.

HABITAT: Rich, moist, humusy, definitely acid soil; shade.

DESCRIPTION: Shiny leathery, evergreen, heart-shaped leaves that turn red to bronze in winter; narrow raceme of tiny white flowers 8 to 18 in. tall.

BLOOM PERIOD: Late spring.

OUTSTANDING FEATURE: An evergreen groundcover without equal for the right place.

NATURAL RANGE: Virginia and West Virginia to Georgia and Alabama.

CULTURE: Coming though it does from the southern mountains, this beauty is hardy at least into central New England. In its homeland, galax is often found in fairly dry open forests, but one must remember the ever present humidity of the Smokies and give it help in climates where summer is hot and dry. Plenty of acid humus when planting will help keep the pH down as well as aid in retaining moisture in the soil. A pine needle mulch is good, too. Although it must have some moisture, it is definitely not a plant for wet places. At one time thousands of the lustrous leaves were picked for the florist trade, but they are not as commonly used nowadays. You can afford to pick a few yourself after you have a good stand growing, but never take more than a few from any one plant. Galax makes a superb groundcover under acid-loving rhododendrons and azaleas. Where the soil has been carefully prepared, it will spread rather quickly into good mats of foliage. The flowers are nothing much, but consider them a bonus to liven what is essentially a foliage plant.

PROPAGATION: By seed in the fall; by division in spring.

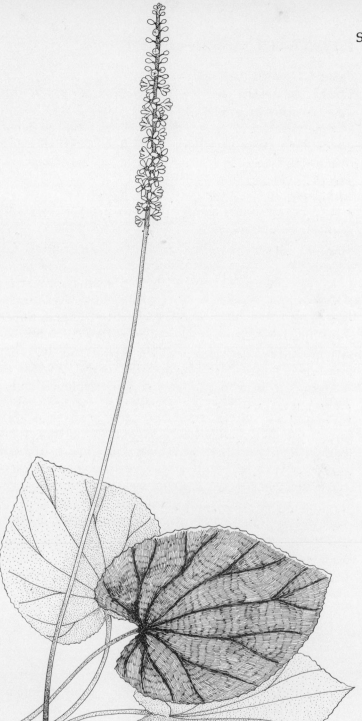

Wandflower (*Galax rotundifolia*)

Wintergreen (*Gaultheria procumbens*)

FAMILY: Heath (*Ericaceae*).
OTHER NICKNAMES: Teaberry, checkerberry, mountain-tea.
HABITAT: Moist, humusy, acid soil; at least partial shade.
DESCRIPTION: 3- to 6-in.-high creeping mats of small evergreen leaves with nodding white bell-shaped flowers followed by large red berries.
BLOOM PERIOD: Early summer.
OUTSTANDING FEATURE: A special delight in winter when leaves and berries are bright against a light snow cover.
NATURAL RANGE: Newfoundland to Manitoba; south to New England, Wisconsin, and Minnesota; to Georgia and Alabama in mountains.
CULTURE: The leaves when bruised have a strong aromatic smell, and once this was the source of wintergreen flavoring. Where the soil is acid and humusy, it will spread rather quickly by underground runners. If you steer the above-ground stems with a few small sticks, you can develop a patch into an attractive groundcover. Without this guidance the plant tends to wander sporadically in long arms. The little urn-shaped bells are not particularly noticeable in the summer because they are rather hidden by the foliage, but the berries are a very bright red and stand out more. Unless birds or children eat them, they are very long-lasting. Sometime last year's berries will still be hanging on when new flowers open. Wintergreen will grow in both partial and full shade, but bloom and the consequent berrying are better in light shade or where the plants get morning sun. The soil for wintergreen should never dry out, but it does not want a wet, low spot either.
RECOMMENDED SELECTION: Var. *macrocarpa* has even larger berries.
RELATED SPECIES: *G. shallon* from the northwest is a much larger plant. Its white to pink bells are borne on a terminal raceme at the end of somewhat arching stems as long as 3 ft. Its berries are purple.
PROPAGATION: Gather and depulp seeds in late winter and sow immediately. Divisions of the runners can be rooted in moist sand and peat, preferably in a terrarium. Also propagate by stem cuttings in summer.

Wintergreen (*Gaultheria procumbens*)

Wild Geranium (*Geranium maculatum*)

FAMILY: Geranium (*Geraniaceae*).

OTHER NICKNAMES: Wood geranium, spotted cranesbill.

HABITAT: Slightly moist, humusy soil; partial shade.

DESCRIPTION: Loose clusters of lavender purple to pink flowers an inch across on 1- to 2-ft. stalks; finely cut leaves.

BLOOM PERIOD: Late spring.

OUTSTANDING FEATURES: An easy plant for open woodland or the edges of a shady garden.

NATURAL RANGE: Maine to Manitoba; south to Georgia, Tennessee, Missouri, and Kansas.

CULTURE: Perhaps we should note first that this plant is a true geranium and not a pelargonium, the so-called geranium sold for flowerbeds and windowboxes by every roadside stand in the spring. This wild geranium is rock hardy and asks little attention. Again, while it is not a dramatic kind of flower, the geranium has a dainty charm. It does not pick well, however. The flower stems bend with any stir in the air so that from a distance a planting seems alive with pinky butterflies. Wild geraniums bloom best if given some sunlight during the day, and where winters are not too harsh the basal foliage is nearly evergreen. These plants grow from a stout rootstock, so don't plant them too closely together. They definitely look best, however, if grown in colonies of at least six plants. They also tend to self-sow. If you mulch the soil around your geraniums so it is weed-free and without much competition from other growing things, you can encourage a small planting to increase all by itself into an effective grouping. A good addition of humus during the initial planting will aid the roots to take a quick hold and help retain moisture during the hotter months. Flowering seems to last longer in spots where the soil does not dry out drastically, but the geranium is not a plant for wet places. In the wild, plants are often found on slopes.

RECOMMENDED SELECTION: A rare white form is sometimes listed and reputedly comes true from seed.

RELATED SPECIES: *G. oreganum* is very similar but found in the wild only in a very limited area in Oregon.

PROPAGATION: By seed; by division in spring, but make sure each piece of root has several eyes.

Wild Geranium (*Geranium maculatum*)

Bowman's-Root (*Gillenia trifoliata*)

FAMILY: Rose (*Rosaceae*).

OTHER NICKNAME: Indian-physic.

HABITAT: Humusy soil on acid side; full to partial shade.

DESCRIPTION: Thready white flowers about an inch across on bushy plants around 3 ft. high; good clean summer foliage.

BLOOM PERIOD: Late spring, early summer.

OUTSTANDING FEATURES: Adds color to shady spots after nearly all other spring blossoms are gone; a good accent plant.

NATURAL RANGE: New York to Ontario and Michigan; south to Georgia and Alabama.

CULTURE: Except that it should be planted in soil with some humus and given water during summers of extreme drought, this unassuming plant asks for very little but offers a great deal for the shaded garden. I have had it grow as well in clay as in woodland soil, but it seems to do best with enough humus to keep soil on the acid side; hence, use peat moss liberally when planting. The little flowers are borne on the ends of the branches, so they are quite showy; and they flutter in the slightest breeze, giving motion to the garden. Sometimes there is a pink tinge to the blossom, and this characteristic would be a good one for someone to do selecting for. Gillenia can be used equally well as an accent plant in the shady garden or among shrubs as long as it gets at least half a day of shadow. If the first blossoms are clipped off before seed sets, there will be additional bloom. Gillenia is hardy north of its natural range. I have never seen pest or disease touch the handsomely cut foliage. A group of plants can be used much like a bush in the shady garden, although it takes a few years of growing to attain bush size.

RELATED SPECIES: *G. stipulata* (American ipecac) is much similar but grows a little taller.

PROPAGATION: By seed; by division in spring.

Bowman's-Root (*Gillenia trifoliata*)

Liverwort (*Hepatica acutiloba*)

FAMILY: Buttercup (*Ranunculaceae*).
OTHER NICKNAME: Sharp-lobed hepatica.
HABITAT: Well-drained, humusy soil; shade.
DESCRIPTION: Low-growing, leathery leaves are evergreen; small flowers on stems a few inches high, may be white, pink, lilac, or blue and have prominent yellow stamens.
BLOOM PERIOD: Early spring.
OUTSTANDING FEATURE: One of the first flowers to appear in spring.
NATURAL RANGE: Maine to Minnesota; south to Georgia, Alabama, and Missouri.
CULTURE: When the furry buds of the hepatica begin to open, the easterner knows that the back of winter is finally broken. I well remember the south-facing bank of a little valley in the woods where I went to look for them as a child. Even with snow still on the ground, spring came first to this warm site, although later in the year most of its was in deep shade from the trees. Try to find a similar location if you would have the earliest hepaticas in your garden. If you cannot duplicate the perfect situation, make sure that the woodsy soil is at least well drained and that there will be shade later in the season before you plant hepaticas. The hepaticas on my childhood bank flowered exceptionally well, so that I am quite certain winter sun is necessary. The common name refers to the shape of the leaves, which resemble a human liver. They turn maroon and brown in winter, and very soon after flowering are replaced by clean green ones. No shady garden should be without these gay harbingers of kinder weather. This species is tolerant as to the type of soil it grows in, being found in neutral to limy sites as well as growing in acid humus.
RECOMMENDED SELECTIONS: A few dealers offer hepaticas by color, which is a delightful way to arrange them in the garden.
RELATED SPECIES: *H. americana* (round-lobed hepatica) differs mainly in that its three lobes are round rather than pointed, but also seems to require a more acid soil. Use plenty of peat moss when preparing the site and mulch with pine needles or leafmold. This hepatica is found in the wild much farther north than its sister.
PROPAGATION: By seed; by division in spring after flowering.

Liverwort (*Hepatica acutiloba*)

Gold Star-Grass (*Hypoxis hirsuta*)

FAMILY: Amaryllis (*Amaryllidaceae*).
OTHER NICKNAMES: Hairy or yellow star-grass, goldeye-grass.
HABITAT: Rich, humusy soil that is on the acid side; partial shade.
DESCRIPTION: Loose clusters of small gold stars on stems a few inches high; foliage grassy.
BLOOM PERIOD: Spring into late fall.
OUTSTANDING FEATURE: One of the longest-flowering plants for the outdoor garden.
NATURAL RANGE: Maine to Manitoba; south to Florida and Texas.
CULTURE: Countless acres are devoted to the cultivation of daffodils (relatives of this diminutive treasure), but you will have to search the catalogs to find a start of hypoxis. And yet the individual daffodil (while admittedly showier) completes its flowering in a few weeks at most. This little native just keeps going until hard frost finally cuts it down. To encourage this long bloom period snip off the old flowers from time to time. More important is to make sure the plants never lack for moisture. Although I have found them in boggy places, in the garden just plant them with plenty of humus, mulch well, and give extra water during drought. Perhaps in the far north or in wet spots they will grow in full sun; in my garden they do best with a touch of afternoon shade at least, and I have one patch that gets only filtered sunshine. Because the plants are so diminutive, hypoxis is best planted in a colony. The tiny bulbs go about an inch deep only and can be planted either in early spring or in fall. Happily, hypoxis will self-sow rather quickly if soil is lightly mulched to keep weeds down. I cannot think of a better plant for a rock garden, and it is also lovely in a woodsy terrarium, where often it will bloom. Southern dealers are more apt to carry the bulbs, but try to find a northern supplier if your winter climate is severe. There are a number of other species locally native to the southeast, and they might not prove as hardy as this one. It is a shame no one has tried to hybridize or select for a slightly bigger flower. While I love its very daintiness, the larger size would probably bring hypoxis the fame it needs. It is the longest-flowering plant I have ever grown.
PROPAGATION: By seed; by division of offsets in late fall.

Gold Star-Grass (*Hypoxis hirsuta*)

Crested Iris (*Iris cristata*)

FAMILY: Iris (*Iridaceae*).
HABITAT: Well-drained, humusy soil; partial shade.
DESCRIPTION: A lavender blue iris with a yellow crest, around 2 in.
across on a stem 4 to 6 in. high; leaves are narrow, and mature
fans seldom top 6 in.
BLOOM PERIOD: Spring.
OUTSTANDING FEATURES: A good groundcover or edging plant for
the shady garden.
NATURAL RANGE: Maryland to Indiana and Missouri; south to
Alabama, Mississippi, and Oklahoma.
CULTURE: Certainly one of the most important native irises for
gardeners, it blooms earlier than many others, is tolerant of many
garden situations, and is really lovely in bloom, with foliage that
is easy to live with afterward. Although a southerner, it is hardy
well into New England and well worth trying anywhere. In the
Philadelphia area *I. cristata* blooms best where it gets a bit of
morning sun but needs afternoon shade to increase nicely and keep
good foliage. I have one clump in high shade all day, and that has
done well, too. Farther north it may do satisfactorily in almost full
sun. This iris spreads by thin rhizomes. Before winter sets in,
shake a thin covering of humusy soil or compost over the wiry
running stems lest they be killed by frost. A group moves ever
outward, so you will have to reset rhizomes every few years to
keep a stand in one spot and prevent crowding.
RECOMMENDED SELECTIONS: Gold Crest and Skylands are named
selections. The lovely white variety is widely offered, and in my
garden has proved more robust than the type—and is gorgeous in
front of red columbine, which blooms at the same time.
RELATED SPECIES: *I. verna*, with pale blue flowers, is even earlier,
smaller, and dwarfer, but requires a thin, very acid soil. *I.
prismatica* wants sandy acid soil but prefers much wetter
situations. Blue-flag (*I. versicolor*) is good for lake and stream
margins. *I. fulva* is the parent of many new Louisiana iris hybrids
with red and copper tones and is hardy quite far north. It likes
moisture. *I. missouriensis* has blue lavender blooms on 15-in.
stems; it likes dry spots and full sun. *I. douglasiana*, from the west
coast, is offered in several colors. It grows about 12 in. tall and
blooms in the shade.
PROPAGATION: By seed; by division of rhizomes after flowering.

Crested Iris *(Iris cristata)*

Twinleaf (*Jeffersonia diphylla*)

FAMILY: Barberry (*Berberidaceae*).
OTHER NICKNAME: Rheumatism-root.
HABITAT: Rich, humusy soil; at least partial shade.
DESCRIPTION: White flowers about an inch across; leaves resemble green butterflies on 1 ft. stems; odd seedpods.
BLOOM PERIOD: Early spring.
OUTSTANDING FEATURE: Foliage adds captivating note to shady garden.
NATURAL RANGE: New York and Ontario to Wisconsin and Iowa; south to Alabama.
CULTURE: Though little known by most gardeners, this plant is beloved by those who grow it. Each flower lasts only a day, but the leaves, which follow, remain decorative for many months, their motion in a breeze bringing life to the cool quiet of the summer woodland. When ripe, the lid of the seedpod lifts up, reminding me of a miniature version of the hinged pipe smoked by Dutch burghers. It is difficult to gather the seed unless one watches the ripening pods constantly. The plants self–sow readily in the right situation, so it is easier to let them do the work and transplant the progeny where wanted in early spring. Incorporate plenty of humus in the soil when planting, and do not let the plants want for moisture in summer to encourage the foliage to last. Twinleaf will prosper in nearly complete summer shade if there is good light. This plant, incidentally, is the symbol of Bowman's Hill State Wildflower Preserve, Washington Crossing Park, Washington Crossing, Pennsylvania. Quite fittingly, this native is named after our third president, who did much to encourage scientific farming and horticulture. The Lewis and Clark expedition he sent out to explore the Louisiana Purchase discovered hundreds of native plants new to botany.
PROPAGATION: By seed; by division in spring.

Twinleaf (*Jeffersonia diphylla*)

Partridge-Berry (*Mitchella repens*)

FAMILY: Madder (*Rubiaceae*).
OTHER NICKNAMES: Twinberry, squawberry.
HABITAT: Moist, humusy, rather acid soil; shade.
DESCRIPTION: A very low evergreen creeper with small round leaves and pairs of tiny, fragrant trumpet flowers in white or pale pink. Each pair of flowers produces one long–lasting red berry.
BLOOM PERIOD: Spring.
OUTSTANDING FEATURE: Attractive groundcover in right situation.
NATURAL RANGE: New Hampshire, Quebec, Ontario, and Minnesota; south to Florida and Texas.
CULTURE: With today's increased interest in terrariums, the partridge–berry has once again come into its own as an indoor decoration. Oldtime New Englanders fancied berry bowls as a way to bring the outdoors inside during the long winter. That lovely custom has been enjoying a renewal, as more indoor gardeners discover that the berries of this tiny charmer will remain red and plump for more than a year in a correctly maintained glass garden. After a season such gardens can be dismantled, and the partridge–berry plants in them transplanted directly to the garden. Use lots of peat moss in the soil where they are to go, mulch lightly with pine needles, and water well and often until you are sure they have made themselves at home. In the north the plants may do well in situations where there is a bit of sun, but full shade is advised in other climates. Locations under pine trees or oaks, where the soil is likely to be acid, are particularly suitable planting sites. Partridge–berry will take drier soil in cool summers, but I try to assure them of some moisture in the soil. In cultivation, berry production is never as good as in the wild but you will get fine mats of foliage. Slug bait may be indicated, especially in warmer climates.
PROPAGATION: Plant the berries in the fall in damp peat and sand. Since the plants root at nearly every node, you can press stem or root cuttings into peat in a terrarium at any season and have dozens of new plants in a short time, but these should be individually potted and kept in the nursery or cold frame for one season.

Partridge-Berry (*Mitchella repens*)

Showy Orchis (*Orchis spectabilis*)

FAMILY: Orchid (*Orchidaceae*).
HABITAT: Rich, moist, humusy soil; shade.
DESCRIPTION: Several fragrant white and purply flowers on a sturdy 5-to 9–in. stalk above two large shiny basal leaves.
BLOOM PERIOD: Spring.
OUTSTANDING FEATURE: A rather spectacular rarity for the cool woodland garden.
NATURAL RANGE: Quebec to Ontario; south to New England, northern Georgia, Tennessee, Missouri and Kansas.
CULTURE: Please don't order this plant unless you are willing to make special attempts to provide a hospitable home. Prepare the site well and deeply with plenty of rich humus such as leafmold added to a well-drained loam. Do an area larger than at first needed, because the roots travel with age. The plants should have definite shade, and good air circulation helps keep down the soil temperature, particularly along its southern limits. You will note it is not a denizen of the hotter states, and a real attempt should be made to pick a site that remains cool in summer. Where it ventures below the Mason–Dixon line, it is in the mountains. I wouldn't even try it in a warm climate. A good mulch and adequate moisture will help, but unless the soil is right, the plants will just give up after a year or so. Since it is often found in calcareous woods, one guesses the showy orchis does not require highly acid soil, but it must have humus. Mulching with marble chips after planting may be wise. One good idea is to choose a possible site and start some bloodroot, red trillium, and maidenhair fern there. If these prosper, you can then add the orchid. Be prepared to protect your orchid against mice, rabbits, and slugs—as well as fleabrains who would pick it, leaves and all, for a bouquet. This treatment will kill the plants as effectively as beheading kills people.
RELATED SPECIES: Sorry, but that's as far as I'll go in suggesting wild orchids for gardens.
PROPAGATION: Division of the tuberlike roots when dormant in fall, but never attempt this without a good reason. If the plant is thriving, leave it alone.

Showy Orchis (*Orchis spectabilis*)

Violet Oxalis (*Oxalis violacea*)

FAMILY: Oxalis (*Oxalidaceae*).
OTHER NICKNAME: Violet wood-sorrel.
HABITAT: Rich, slightly acid, humusy soil; partial shade.
DESCRIPTION: Small lavender flowers grow on stems 4 to 6 in. high above rather dainty shamrocklike leaves.
BLOOM PERIOD: Spring and early summer.
OUTSTANDING FEATURES: Incredibly easy to establish a colony.
NATURAL RANGE: Florida to New Mexico; north to Massachusetts, New York, Ohio, Indiana, Wisconsin, Minnesota, North Dakota, and Colorado.
CULTURE: Be forewarned by that phrase "incredibly easy." This is not a plant for the small garden full of rare treasures. Given halfway decent woodsy soil, oxalis multiplies rapidly by runners from little bulbs. Where you want an underplanting for shrubs or trees that needs no pampering, this might be a good choice. There are never lots of flowers, and it may look hauntingly like the pesky yellow sorrel that is a weed all over the northeast. Nevertheless there is some merit in its ease of culture and hardiness. Larger woodland plants can easily compete with the oxalis, so you can have this and them, too. Just remember that it does spread and can become a pest itself in the wrong place.
RELATED SPECIES: *O. montana* (common wood-sorrel) is a plant only for very acid, humusy woodland in cool northern climates. It bears quite striking white flowers, not quite an inch across, that are veined with pink.
PROPAGATION: By division in spring.

Violet Oxalis (*Oxalis violacea*)

Woodland Phlox (*Phlox divaricata*)

FAMILY: Phlox (*Polemoniaceae*).
OTHER NICKNAMES: May or blue phlox, wild sweet William.
HABITAT: Humusy soil; partial shade.
DESCRIPTION: Small clusters of fragrant blue to lavender flowers borne 6 to 18 in. high; evergreen foliage only a few inches high.
BLOOM PERIOD: Spring.
OUTSTANDING FEATURE: One of the best woodland groundcovers.
NATURAL RANGE: Quebec to Manitoba; south to Florida and Louisiana.
CULTURE: With partial shade and a woodsy soil, this lovely native will slowly spread into wonderful colonies. Rooting is shallow, and a mulch helps. Hardy bulbs can easily be planted between the phlox. Like all members of the family, it is a prime target for hungry rabbits, but no other pest is important. If necessary, fence your plantings with low, inconspicuous baskets of chicken wire. If the site is not too dry, woodland phlox will do very nicely in a spot that is sunny in spring but gets shade later from deciduous trees. This phlox blooms well, however, in shady spots, and no woodland garden should be without it.
RECOMMENDED SELECTIONS: There is a fine pure white form, as well as var. *laphami*, which has deeper blue flowers and unnotched petals.
RELATED SPECIES: *P. pilosa* (prairie or downy phlox) is equally hardy and somewhat similar but not as good a groundcover. Its pink flowers appear just after May phlox stops blooming, and it takes rather dry situations. *P. amoena* (hairy phlox) has salmon pink blossoms seldom higher than 6 in. Sometimes called mountain pink, it also does well with more sun. Although a more southerly species, it is reported hardy in New England. Several other excellent native phloxes are described in the sunny plant section. There are many western species that are seldom seen in commerce, but there is no reason not to try any local to your area in your own garden. I have never grown a phlox I didn't love.
PROPAGATION: By seed. There is always some variation in color and flower size. Division in spring, however, is the preferred method and much quicker.

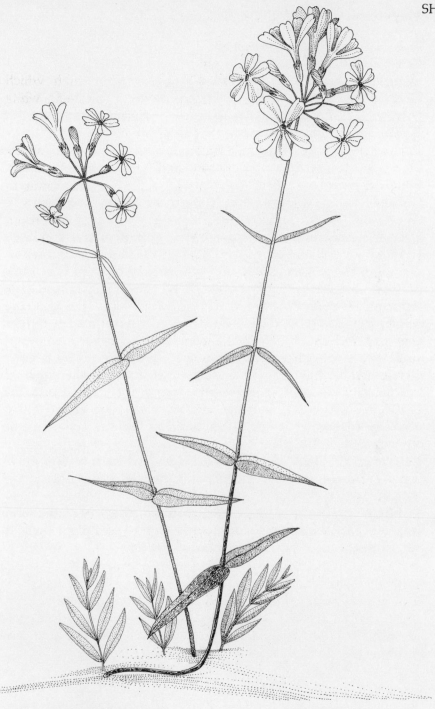

Woodland Phlox (*Phlox divaricata*)

May-Apple (*Podophyllum peltatum*)

FAMILY: Barberry (*Berberidaceae*).

OTHER NICKNAME: Mandrake.

HABITAT: Almost any soil with some humus; shade.

DESCRIPTION: Large, deeply divided leaves 1 ft. high which resemble an unfolding umbrella in early spring; nodding white flower almost hidden under leaves; yellow fall berry.

BLOOM PERIOD: Late spring.

OUTSTANDING FEATURE: A groundcover for difficult shady situations where nothing else is wanted.

NATURAL RANGE: Quebec and Ontario to Minnesota; south to Florida and Texas.

CULTURE: You could kill a May-apple if you planted it in full sun and very dry soil, but otherwise I'd bet on the plant. Given enough humus in the soil and some moisture, it will take quite a lot of sunshine, but it is naturally a plant of the open woods. Were it less rampant, we might treasure it, but the plain truth is that it spreads rapidly by underground roots and after only a few years will take over any area in which it gets a start. I would never plant May-apple in a small garden, but there are sometimes problem areas such as narrow shady fringes of driveways or slopes where erosion is a danger. In such a spot this plant can be introduced with full confidence that it will survive and cover the bare earth. If you need to encourage it on those problem banks, spread some humusy mulch after planting and water well until growth starts or the leaves no longer wilt. A few rocks will help hold the soil initially. I have even successfully transplanted May-apple in full growth.

PROPAGATION: In the unlikely event you don't have enough plants very quickly, rub the seeds out of the berries and plant them in fall. Rootstocks may be divided almost any time.

May-Apple (*Podophyllum peltatum*)

Jacob's-Ladder (*Polemonium reptans*)

FAMILY: Phlox (*Polemoniaceae*).

OTHER NICKNAME: Greek-valerian.

HABITAT: Rich, humusy soil; partial shade.

DESCRIPTION: Clusters of small blue bells on 1-ft. stems above somewhat ferny foliage.

BLOOM PERIOD: Spring.

OUTSTANDING FEATURES: Creates a fine splash of blue. Where moisture is adequate, foliage remains decorative all summer.

NATURAL RANGE: New York to Minnesota; south to Georgia, Mississippi, Missouri, and Oklahoma.

CULTURE: If this were the only member of this genus, we could rest content, for it is tolerant of a variety of garden conditions and rewards its grower twofold because the mature leaves are so delicately decorative all by themselves. Farther north the plants may well grow in nearly full sun, but in my Pennsylvania garden afternoon shade is a must to keep the foliage healthy. In bloom a mature plant gives a fountainlike effect and contrasts especially well with primroses and daffodils. This native does not creep, despite its specific name, but it does self-sow. Use plenty of humus in planting because summer heat makes the leaves wilt; give a good soaking during dry periods. Plants which do an adequate job of leaf production also seem to bloom better. *P. reptans* is also good for slightly moist places which get high tree shade. There is considerable variation in the blue of various plants, and it is a shame no one has made any selections of our natives, which are much lovelier than the European species so often touted.

RELATED SPECIES: *P. van-bruntiae* of the northeast blooms later, has purply flowers, and can reach 30 in. The western states have many other good polemoniums. *P. delicatum* is a 4-in. dwarf, while *P. pulcherrimum* ranges from 6 to 12 in.; both are beloved by rock gardeners, very hardy, and do well in humusy soil. *P. mellitum* is a white from the Rockies. *P. carneum* from the Pacific northwest has somewhat funnel-shaped flowers and is called the varicolored Jacob's-ladder because its blossoms start out salmon or yellow and change to pink shades. It blooms most of the summer if grown in cool, moist shade with the old flowers removed before seed sets. It is a breathtaking plant.

PROPAGATION: By seed; by division in the spring.

Jacob's-Ladder (*Polemonium reptans*)

Gay-Wings (*Polygala paucifolia*)

FAMILY: Milkwort (*Polygalaceae*).
OTHER NICKNAMES: Fringed milkwort, flowering wintergreen, bird-on-the-wing.
HABITAT: Rich, humusy, very acid soil; shade.
DESCRIPTION: A few small purply pink flowers with a prominent fringed crest on creeping stems only a few inches tall; leaves may be evergreen.
BLOOM PERIOD: Late spring to early summer.
OUTSTANDING FEATURES: Incredibly beautiful but difficult.
NATURAL RANGE: Quebec to Manitoba; south to inland Virginia, mountains of Georgia, Tennessee, Illinois, and Minnesota.
CULTURE: Another challenging plant that is better left to the experts unless you have a cool, very acid soil garden. As you can see by its range, this is not a plant for hot climates. Used as a groundcover (it spreads slowly) under rhododendrons and other acid-loving shrubs, it is a real treasure. Slugs are one of the worst enemies, so use bait under some rocks nearby. This plant seems to benefit from the cool of the rocks for its roots and is often found on slopes well scattered with rock formations. Note that such sites also guarantee good drainage. A pine–needle mulch is helpful. Those of us who have seen colonies of fringed polygala under the mountain–laurels of the Poconos can only wonder at the glory of nature; the plant seldom attains such proportions in gardens even when conditions are to its liking. Most experts insist on some of the original soil being left with the roots when transplanting; often there are soil organisms present that the plant must have.
RECOMMENDED SELECTION: There is a rare pure white form.
RELATED SPECIES: *P. senega* (Seneca snakeroot) is a quite different species and seems to prefer neutral to limy soil. From its woody rootstock arise stems 6 to 15 in. tall, each with a cone-shaped cluster of small whitish flowers at the top. Many other milkworts are annuals or biennials.
PROPAGATION: By seed sown as soon as it is ripe. Stem cuttings from new growth in early summer will root in sandy acid peat in a terrarium, but leave for a year to get a good root system.

Gay-Wings (*Polygala paucifolia*)

Great Solomon-Seal (*Polygonatum commutatum*)

FAMILY: Lily (*Liliaceae*).
OTHER NAME: *P. canaliculatum.*
HABITAT: Rich, moist, humusy soil; shade.
DESCRIPTION: Clusters of several small creamy bells hang beneath the leaves on tall arching stems 3 to 8 ft. high; bluish berries in fall.
BLOOM PERIOD: Late spring.
OUTSTANDING FEATURES: Foliage stays green all summer; makes excellent accent note on shady garden.
NATURAL RANGE: New Hampshire to Manitoba; south to South Carolina, Tennessee, Missouri, and Oklahoma.
CULTURE: Choose this species if you have a large shaded area; in smaller gardens either of the species below is more likely to be in proportion. All are easy and real contributions to the woodland garden or even a fairly well–shaded border. *P. commutatum* reaches its greatest heights in very rich, damp ground, but I would never plant it in a wet site. Neither the flowers nor the berries are particularly showy, but the arching stems add really good interest to a shady spot. The popular name arises from the fact that the creeping underground stems bear seal-like scars where branches from former years originated. Use plenty of humus when planting, mulch well, and give extra water in summer if there is no rain to keep the foliage clean and green. Solomon-seals often sulk after transplanting. Leave the site alone for another full growing season before giving up. They may well appear the second year after no sign at all the first.
RELATED SPECIES: Smooth Solomon-seal (*P. biflorum*) is a smaller version of its great sister, seldom topping 3 ft. *P. pubescens* (hairy Solomon-seal) is so named because the leaves are downy underneath. Both tend to bear their flowers in pairs, like a slightly acid soil, and grow where it is considerably drier in nature. These two are also very hardy. All three have leaves that look pleated.
PROPAGATION: By seed; by division in early spring.

Great Solomon-Seal (*Polygonatum commutatum*)

Bloodroot (*Sanguinaria canadensis*)

FAMILY: Poppy (*Papaveraceae*).
OTHER NICKNAMES: Red puccoon, puccoon-root, red Indian paint.
HABITAT: Rich, well-drained loam; half shade.
DESCRIPTION: Fairly large white starry flowers with prominent yellow stamens on stems to 8 in. high; silvery green leaves.
BLOOM PERIOD: Early spring.
OUTSTANDING FEATURE: An easy, delightful spring harbinger.
NATURAL RANGE: Quebec to Manitoba; south to Florida and Texas.
CULTURE: Wherever there is humusy soil and summer shade, the bloodroot will make itself at home and gladden the heart of every passerby in early spring. The flowers have a satiny glow in sunshine, and plants seem to prefer spots where there is sunshine during the time they blossom. Put them, therefore, on the eastern edges of the shady garden, under deciduous trees or even in the border where later plants will cast shadow. I mulch mine well and even water them if late spring is dry to keep the leaves growing as long as possible. This gives vigor to the spreading rootstocks. Under such care you can soon have a good-sized colony. Indians used the red juice of the roots as dye, and a drop on a lump of sugar was an oldtime cough remedy. Picked flowers drop the petals almost at once, so allow yours to set seed instead. Once in a while a patch of bloodroot will just disappear, and I blame mice, but without any real proof of their depredations. Sometimes pink-tinged blossoms are found, but no selection of such have been made so far.
RECOMMENDED SELECTIONS: As early as 1732 semidouble forms were described, and you may notice some flowers with extra petals. The real treasure, however, is is the true double. Variously cataloged as var. *multiplex* or *flore plena*, it is for me a vigorous plant that has spread into a fine colony underneath a dogwood tree. The very double flowers are sterile, so last longer than the singles. They resemble tiny waterlilies, and to see one is to covet it immediately. The price of a start is steep, but I consider it one of the very best investments ever made for my garden.
PROPAGATION: Single forms by seed; all by division of the thick creeping rootstock in fall after the leaves dry up. Let the cut pieces scab overnight before replanting.

Bloodroot (*Sanguinaria canadensis*)

Early Saxifrage (*Saxifraga virginiensis*)

FAMILY: Rockfoil (*Saxifragaceae*).

OTHER NICKNAMES: Virginia or eastern saxifrage.

HABITAT: Well-drained, humusy soil amid rocks; partial shade.

DESCRIPTION: Clusters of tiny white stars on hairy stems 4 to 12 in. high above basal rosette of fleshy foliage.

BLOOM PERIOD: Early spring.

OUTSTANDING FEATURE: Probably the easiest saxifrage to grow.

NATURAL RANGE: Quebec to Ontario and Minnesota; south to Georgia, Tennessee, and Missouri.

CULTURE: There are many saxifrages. Those from European sources and those native to the western mountains are the delight and the despair of the advanced rock gardener, for they are not easy plants to make at home outside their alpine homes. This easterner is the exception. Saxifrage means "rock breaker," a good hint as to the natural haunts of such plants. They like to get their roots down into the cool, moist crevices of rocks. Since they want perfect drainage but adequate moisture, they are most apt to be found on damp slopes rather than in flatland. You can provide a few rocks and a slightly raised area at the edge of some trees to make this one quite at home. It is much more tolerant of some soil acidity than many of its relatives, but use some marble chips as mulch if in doubt. Slugs can be pests, however. Partial shade, especially in summer, is wise from Pennsylvania south.

RELATED SPECIES: *S. leucanthemifolia* (*michauxi*) from more southern states has larger leaves, taller flower stems, and wants partial shade. *S. pensylvanica* (swamp saxifrage) actually does grow in wet, fairly sunny places, has heads of flowers borne 3 ft. high which are greenish white.

PROPAGATION: By seed; by division in spring.

Early Saxifrage *(Saxifraga virginiensis)*

Mountain Stonecrop (*Sedum ternatum*)

FAMILY: Orpine (*Crassulaceae*).
OTHER NICKNAMES: Three-leaved or triplet stonecrop, pepper-and-salt.
HABITAT: Well-drained, humusy soil; likes rocky ledges; at least partial shade.
DESCRIPTION: A prostrate evergreen succulent seldom higher than 6 in. with flat sprays of starry white flowers.
BLOOM PERIOD: Spring.
OUTSTANDING FEATURE: Groundcover for shady slopes or rock gardens.
NATURAL RANGE: New York to Michigan and Illinois; south to Georgia and Tennessee.
CULTURE: At least in warmer states, this sedum will luxuriate in nearly full shade. While it does spread by means of creeping stems, it is not anywhere as invasive as so many other sedums. To me the open sprays of blossoms are also more graceful than the round clusters produced by many of the more common sedums. It seems tolerant of ordinary garden soil, but it must have plenty of humus and mulch if in a dry spot. The whorls of three leaves are quite pretty growing down a rock. I am not sure I would put this one in a small choice rock garden, but in a larger planting this sedum is a good selection for shady portions, especially since it remains nearly evergreen. It is hardy north of its natural range.
RELATED SPECIES: *S. telephoides* (Allegheny stonecrop) bears round heads of pink flowers in late summer and likes the same rocky situation but with more sun. Its interesting purply foliage is often 1 ft. tall. Be forewarned, however, for it has names like wild live-forever and is a fast spreader. *S. nevi* from Virginia's mountains is a tiny gem, wants acid soil, bears white flowers 4 in. high above dense leaf rosettes. Rock garden specialists carry some western mountaineers. *S. purdyi* has white flowers 4 in. high above flat leaf rosettes and is mat-forming by means of red stolons. It wants partial shade. *S. spathulifolium* forms evergreen mats 2 in. high, has yellow flowers on 3-in. stems, and takes some sun. Its var. Capo-Blanco is a 2-in. dwarf with silvery white leaf rosettes.
PROPAGATION: By seed; by division in spring.

Mountain Stonecrop (*Sedum ternatum*)

Oconee-Bells (*Shortia galacifolia*)

FAMILY: Diapensia (*Diapensiaceae*).

HABITAT: Moist but well-drained sandy, very acid soil with good humus content; shade.

DESCRIPTION: White or pinkish bell-like flowers about an inch across on stalks 3 to 6 in. high; shiny evergreen leaves turn bronze and red in fall.

BLOOM PERIOD: Spring.

OUTSTANDING FEATURES: A simply beautiful flower and ground-cover.

NATURAL RANGE: Mountains of North Carolina.

CULTURE: Although native to a very small area in the south, this plant is hardy well into New England. Indeed, shortia is easier to cultivate there than in more southerly places, because it wants cool growing conditions. Some filtered sunlight may be possible in Massachusetts, but in a warmer climate shortia needs full shade. My friends around Philadelphia who are successful with it have it in sites that face toward the north. While the plants do spread into colonies by means of short runners, they do not do this with any speed. I consider shortia well worth the extra trouble of preparing a special niche for it. Mix leafmold and sphagnum with coarse sand so that the pH is 4–5. A pine-needle mulch will help, too. Make sure the spot is not one where water with any lime content (from a sidewalk or building foundation) will flow. This is, incidentally, the famous "lost flower" of American botany. The first report of its existence was disbelieved until a subsequent discovery of plants many years later finally confirmed the earlier description. Although shortia grows in a very limited area in the wild, it is widely offered by wildflower specialists, partly because of its beauty and partly because of demand by cognoscenti. The fact remains that it tolerates only a very specific environment. If you are not willing to meet those strict requirements, I beg you not to buy it.

PROPAGATION: Difficult from seed; division after spring flowering; early summer cuttings grown in sandy acid medium.

Oconee-Bells (*Shortia galacifolia*)

Solomon-Plume (*Smilacina racemosa*)

FAMILY: Lily (*Liliaceae*).
OTHER NICKNAMES: False Solomon-seal, false spikenard.
HABITAT: Rich, slightly acid, humusy soil; shade.
DESCRIPTION: Tiny starry white flowers in a terminal cluster on an arching, nicely leaved stem 2 to 3 ft. high; red berries.
BLOOM PERIOD: Late spring.
OUTSTANDING FEATURES: Flower, foliage, and berries all showy.
NATURAL RANGE: Quebec to British Columbia; south to Virginia, Tennessee, and Missouri.
CULTURE: If you were to dig up and compare the roots, those of this near-cousin of the Solomon-seal would not show any scars. The flowers and berries are quite different, too, but the good clean foliage does resemble that of polygonatum. In a small garden where you must choose one or the other, this would be my selection because it has more interest during the entire growing season. The clusters of red berries are a bright fall note. To help it get a good start, incorporate plenty of humus into ordinary or sandy loam. When summers are dry, smilacina definitely benefits from extra watering. Otherwise the leaves get rather ratty by summer's end. Farther north it may take filtered shade, but in southeastern Pennsylvania it does well in complete shadow after the trees leaf out. (This is one reason shade-loving natives are such good additions to a home property. They delight in those areas under trees where grass struggles because of lack of sun. Give up on the grass and convert such places to a woodland garden instead.)
RELATED SPECIES: *S. stellata* (starry Solomon-plume) has fewer, larger flowers in a cylindrical head and seldom tops 1 ft. It spreads well by underground stems, so makes a good highish groundcover in shade. Bog Solomon-plume (*S. trifolia*) is even smaller of stature and only for cold, wet, very acid gardens. There are several western species seldom offered commercially.
PROPAGATION: By seeds separated from pulp and sown immediately; by division in spring.

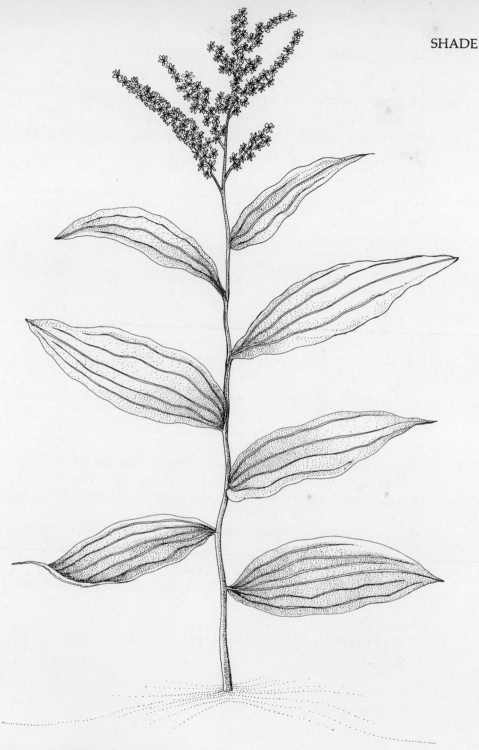

Solomon-Plume (*Smilacina racemosa*)

Celandine Poppy (*Stylophorum diphyllum*)

FAMILY: Poppy (*Papaveraceae*).

OTHER NICKNAMES: Gold-poppy, yellow wood-poppy.

HABITAT: Rich, humusy, moist soil; partial shade.

DESCRIPTION: Loose clusters of yellow poppies 2 in. across above grayish, deeply cut foliage 1 ft. high.

BLOOM PERIOD: Spring and into early summer under favorable conditions.

OUTSTANDING FEATURE: A lovely colonizer under deciduous trees.

NATURAL RANGE: Pennsylvania to Wisconsin; south to Virginia, Tennessee, and Missouri.

CULTURE: Another native that has been sadly neglected by both gardeners and dealers in wild plants. A patch of these bright sunny flowers beside a colony of woodland phlox will quite take your breath away. A most glorious planting of celandine poppies exists at Bowman's Hill State Wildflower Preserve in Pennsylvania. They are situated on a slight south-facing bank, where the soil is rich and fairly moist in spring and where the sun warms the earth early. Later the soil becomes somewhat dry and the shade of the trees is quite dark, but the gold-poppies are quite happy. Their annual duty is done, and they disappear entirely before summer is well along. They have spread both by seed and by creeping roots into a great blanket of color in their season. In spots with slightly more moisture and less shade, the plants will keep going longer, especially if the first furry seed pods are removed before maturing. Because of the spreading underground stems, it would be unwise to plant these in the very small garden, but as an underplanting under large shrubs or trees few plants will make as gay a picture. To ensure enough moisture, incorporate extra humus into the soil when planting if necessary, and mulch with some organic substance. Do not confuse this native with the inferior European celandine (*Chelidonium majus*), which has smaller flowers and much weedier propensities.

PROPAGATION: By seed sown in fall; by division in spring.

222

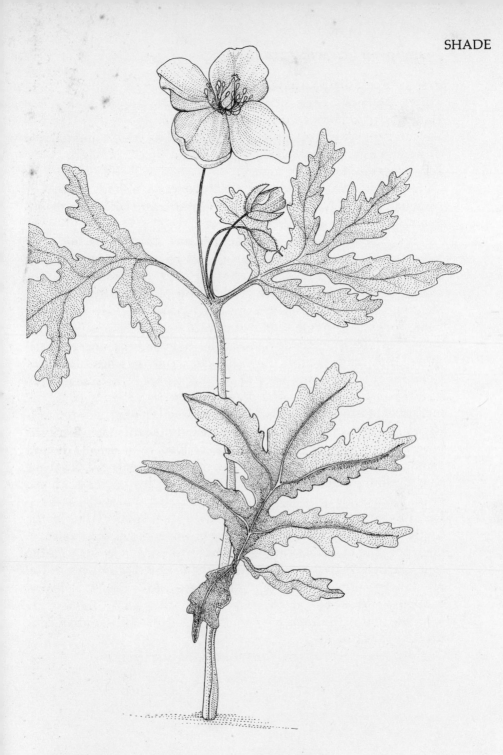

Celandine Poppy (*Stylophorum diphyllum*)

Foamflower (*Tiarella cordifolia*)

FAMILY: Rockfoil (*Saxifragiaceae*).

OTHER NICKNAME: False miterwort.

HABITAT: Rich, humusy soil; cool shade.

DESCRIPTION: A creeping plant with maplelike leaves and narrow clusters of tiny white flowers on stalks from 6 to 12 in. high.

BLOOM PERIOD: Spring.

OUTSTANDING FEATURE: A good groundcover for a shady garden.

NATURAL RANGE: New Brunswick to Ontario and Michigan; south to North Carolina and Tennessee.

CULTURE: Like so many woodland plants, this native will take more sun in northern states, but it must have good shade as you garden farther south. It is a plant of the mountains rather than the coastal areas of the southern states. Add plenty of humus when planting, and do not let it want for moisture in dry summers. Some rocks to provide a cool root run are also helpful in hotter areas. Left to its own devices in the right habitat, tiarella will spread by underground runners into large patches. In some locations the leaves are more or less evergreen. The foliage often turns bronze in the fall. The popular name was suggested by the myriad of foamy stamens sticking out of each flower.

RECOMMENDED HYBRID: By crossing the tiarella with a heuchera the bigeneric hybrid heucherella was created in Europe. It has characteristics intermediate between the two parents. At least one named clone, Bright Bloom, is available in this country. I have heard there is a white one, too.

RELATED SPECIES: *T. wherryi* is a magnificent form found in the southern states but perfectly hardy into the mid-Atlantic states. It does not spread by stolons, so is easier to keep in bounds in the small garden. It has pinkish tints in the flowers. Moreover, if the old flowers are faithfully cut off before seed sets, *T. wherryi* continues flowering much longer than the white species. *T. trifoliata* and *T. unifolia* are both species from the woodlands of the Pacific northwest.

PROPAGATION: By seed sown in fall; by division in spring.

Foamflower (*Tiarella cordifolia*)

Great Trillium (*Trillium grandiflorum*)

FAMILY: Lily (*Liliaceae*).

OTHER NICKNAMES: Wake-robin, trinity-lily, large-flowered trillium.

HABITAT: Rich, well-drained, humusy soil; partial shade.

DESCRIPTION: Showy white flowers 3 to 4 in. across on stems up to 18 in. tall.

BLOOM PERIOD: Spring.

OUTSTANDING FEATURE: Excellent, easy standout for shade.

NATURAL RANGE: Maine and Quebec to Minnesota; south to Georgia and Arkansas.

CULTURE: No shady garden should be without this beauty, but do not ever pick it. The three leaves which so perfectly set off the flowers are the only source of nourishment the underground tuber gets. If they are removed early in spring, that root will not produce a flower the following year and may even give up the ghost entirely. Left to do its duty, however, healthy foliage leads to an increase of roots. For this reason locate your trilliums so they get some filtered sunlight in spring, and encourage the foliage to stay green as long as possible. Extra humus in the soil when planting and addition of an annual thin organic mulch help. So does extra watering when late spring is dry. In nature this trillium if often found in drifts on wooded slopes. It is very picturesque in such a setting, but it is equally perfect as an accent plant in the small garden. Flowers of this white species gradually turn pink as they mature.

RECOMMENDED SELECTION: The pure white double form resembles a gardenia and is a rare treasure.

RELATED SPECIES: The western *T. ovatum* is similar and easy to grow. Of the twenty or so other American trilliums, the next best for gardens is *T. erectum*, which has white, red, and yellow forms and is slightly smaller. *T. nivale* (snow trillium), an early white miniature, prefers limy soil. The toad trilliums (*T. sessile*, *T. luteum*) are more noteworthy for their mottled foliage than their flowers. Nodding trilliums such as *T. cernuum* and *T. flexipes* are less decorative because the flowers are nearly hidden beneath the leaves. The beautiful *T. undulatum* (painted trillium), requires a very acid, cool site.

PROPAGATION: By seed; by division when dormant.

Great Trillium (*Trillium grandiflorum*)

Great Merrybells (*Uvularia grandiflora*)

FAMILY: Lily (*Liliaceae*).
OTHER NICKNAMES: Bellwort, strawbell.
HABITAT: Well-drained, rich, neutral soil; at least partial shade.
DESCRIPTION: Bright yellow nodding bells on stalks 1 to 2 ft. tall; clean foliage that is attractive all summer.
BLOOM PERIOD: SPRING.
OUTSTANDING FEATURE: Excellent accent for shady garden.
NATURAL RANGE: Quebec to North Dakota; south to Georgia, Arkansas, and Oklahoma.
CULTURE: This genus received its scientific name from a fancied resemblance of the pendant bells to the uvula of the palate. I suppose botanists must get inspiration where they can, but the common name is much more apropos. A mature clump is simply marvelous in flower. Myriads of bells move in the slightest breeze, while the green perfoliate leaves give a cool note in summer. The farther south you try to grow it, the cooler a situation you should try to find. Good air circulation and full shade plus some humus in the soil and a rock or marble–chip mulch all help. In our temperate climate we put it under deciduous trees where it gets filtered sun in spring but complete shadow all day during the hot months. I have seen it prosper also on the north side of a building where it got good light but no hot sun. The lime leaking from the mortar of the foundation can help maintain a neutral soil in acid areas. When clumps develop into big masses, they are probably best separated, but replant immediately and not too close together so they need not be disturbed often. This merrybells species is quite good enough to feature in any garden situation where there is considerable shade.
RELATED SPECIES: *U. perfoliata* has forking stems up to 20 in. tall and silvery green leaves oddly placed so the main stem appears to grow right through them. *U. sessile* (wild-oats) is shorter, bears smaller, mostly solitary, pale yellow flowers and spreads into fine patches in humusy woodland. Both these species want soil on the acid side.
PROPAGATION: Seed gathered from the odd triangular capsules is best sown in fall; by division in spring or fall.

Great Merrybells (*Uvularia grandiflora*)

Smooth Yellow Violet (*Viola pensylvanica*)

FAMILY: Violet (*Violaceae*).
OTHER NAME: Botanically also sometimes called *V. eriocarpa.*
HABITAT: Rich, humusy soil; partial shade.
DESCRIPTION: A yellow violet borne on leafy stems as high as 1 ft.; foliage heart-shaped.
BLOOM PERIOD: Spring into early summer.
OUTSTANDING FEATURE: A free-blooming species for shade.
NATURAL RANGE: Nova Scotia to Manitoba; south to Georgia and Texas.
CULTURE: This leaf-stemmed species will quickly make itself at home in woodsy soil. It blooms best if given filtered sunlight and should not dry out unduly. Most of the shade–loving violets want a cool situation but will take considerable sun if moisture is adequate. They will bloom in half-shade and consequently are ideal to establish under trees or on the edge of the shady garden. Like most plants listed in this section, the smooth yellow violet self–sows freely.
RELATED SPECIES: *V. pubescens* (hairy yellow) will take more shade. *V. canadensis* (Canada) resembles the hairy yellow, but flowers are white. *V. rostrata* (long-spurred) has unusual blue-violet flowers; plants are also leaf-stemmed. *V. conspersa* (American dog) is a good leaf–stemmed blue violet for moist spots. *V. hastata* (triangle-leaf) likes it drier. Several stemless violets (they have no leaves on the flower stalk) are good garden companions. *V. palmata* (early blue) has deep violet flowers and finely cut leaves and is very much recommended. *V. lanceolata* (lance-leaved) and *V. primulifolia* (primrose-leaved) are both stemless whites that like moist spots and spread by runners. *V. cucullata* (blue marsh) grows in wet bogs. *V. rotundifolia* (early yellow) is a stemless dwarf and wants wet, acid soil and shade.
PROPAGATION: By seed for all species. Those with runners or multiple crowns are easily divided in spring. Root cuttings are sometimes used. Watch out for violets that produce cleistogamous (closed, self–fertilizing) flowers after the showy blooms. You will find these green seedpods below the leaves. Oddly enough, these growths never have an open flower and just produce seed. Such species are likely to spread all over the garden. Those which have runners can also get out of bounds quickly in the small garden.

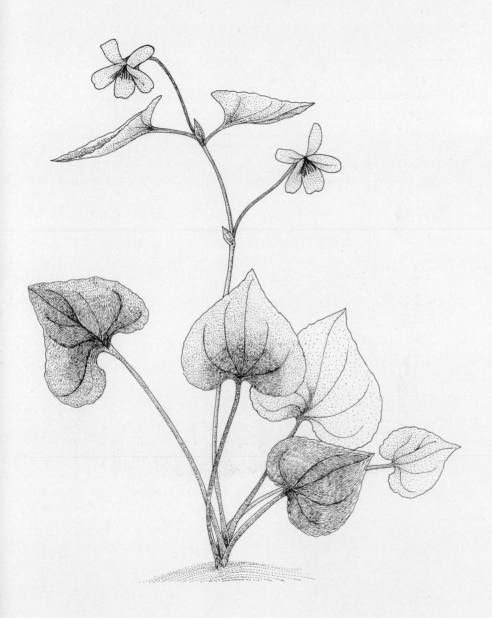

Smooth Yellow Violet (*Viola pensylvanica*)

7
Plants for Wet Spots

In the wild the plants in this section inhabit moist situations —swamps or wet meadows, along streams, or on the verge of ponds and lakes. A few, all members of the waterlily family, actually grow right in the water. Many others, however, are less demanding of their riparian rights. Given reasonable moisture in soil with plenty of water-retaining humus and the aid of a good mulch, they can make themselves comfortably at home far from the water's edge. Some of the most adaptable genera for moist gardens will even be found in the discussions of plants for sun or shade; others are mentioned under the related species listing of main plant entries. If your property needs many plants for wet conditions, consult the Index for the following:

Aruncus dioicus
Asarum sp.
Asclepias incarnata
Aster nova-angliae
Aster puniceus
Claytonia sp.
Coreopsis rosea
Eupatorium coelestinum
Eupatorium purpureum
Helenium autumnale
Iris sp.

Monarda didyma
Phlox maculata
Phlox paniculata
Physostegia virginiana
Podophyllum peltatum
Saxifraga pensylvanica
Smilacina trifolia
Solidago graminifolia
Veronicastrum virginicum
Viola sp.

Summer Aconite (*Aconitum uncinatum*)

FAMILY: Buttercup (*Ranunculaceae*).

OTHER NICKNAMES: Clambering or wild monkshood, wild wolfsbane.

HABITAT: Damp, moderately acid soil; partial shade.

DESCRIPTION: Sparse groups of blue, hooded flowers on weak stems 3 to 5 ft. long; more like a vine.

BLOOM PERIOD: Late summer.

OUTSTANDING FEATURE: An oddity for a half-shaded moist spot.

NATURAL RANGE: Pennsylvania to Indiana; south to Georgia and Alabama.

CULTURE: Varieties of Chinese aconites are much more decorative in the garden itself. This native species is best used to add interest in spots where you have moisture-loving bushes. There it gives a bit of color at the end of the summer when most shrubs are quite through flowering. Truth is, this plant cannot stand "on its own two legs." Rather, it needs some stouter plant to lean on and clamber over. I have found it intriguing, if far from spectacular, growing with some clethra bushes, which like the same damp problem situations. The leaves of the shrubs give the aconite all the shade it requires. Both plants benefit from extra water in dry summers. Note that, like many of its buttercup relatives, the aconite is poisonous in all its parts. Teach your children never to nibble on any strange plant. This business of eating off the wilderness can be risky as well as counter to all conservation practices. Grow or buy your vegetables, and you'll be a lot safer. (So will the woods.)

RELATED SPECIES: *A. noveboracense* (New York monkshood) is a slightly more northern species but very similar except that its stems tend to be hairy.

PROPAGATION: By seed; by division in spring, but aconites dislike being transplanted and often sulk a season after such treatment.

Summer Aconite (*Aconitum uncinatum*)

Jack-in-the-Pulpit (*Arisaema triphyllum*)

FAMILY: Arum (*Araceae*).

OTHER NICKNAMES: Indian-turnip, bog-onion, petit prêcheur.

HABITAT: Deep, rich, humusy soil; part shade; must not dry out.

DESCRIPTION: A green–and–brown–striped spathe flower with a clublike spadix nearly hidden inside; lustrous three-parted leaves 1 to 3 ft. high; red fall berries.

BLOOM PERIOD: Spring.

OUTSTANDING FEATURE: When well grown, gives a tropical look to the shady garden.

NATURAL RANGE: Massachusetts to New York; south to Kentucky and Florida.

CULTURE: In the proper soil and with adequate moisture these interesting plants with huge lush leaves can truly look like something from the jungles. To make Jack "speak," gently rub the bottom of the spathe between your fingers, and squeaky noises will entertain your children. In soil too thin and dry the plants usually refuse to flower or at best wither and disappear during summer without ever producing their heads of bright red berries. Incorporate lots of humus before planting the bulbs and choose a low spot where you can easily water in summer if you do not have a really dampish condition. Handle bulbs with gloves, because they contain a very irritating substance.

RELATED SPECIES: *A. atrorubens* and *A. stewardsoni* are very similar but have a wider natural range north and west. Only a botanist would care about the differences. *A. pulsillum* (swamp Jack) takes very wet, acid sites. *A. dracontium* (greendragon) is a 2- to 3-ft. oddity that takes slightly drier conditions than any of the others. Its spadix extends like a long spike quite far beyond the top of the tubular outer bract and reminds me of a bayonet. Children adore it. It has orange berries, and its one leaf is divided into numerous segments in an arch. Birds collect the berries quite quickly, so if you want a patch to increase, gather them in the fall after they are nice and plump, squash open, and plant the seeds outdoors immediately.

PROPAGATION: By seed as detailed above. I have successfully transplanted these arums in very early spring just as soon as a shoot pops up to show the location of the bulbs, but this must be done carefully, since the bulbs can be quite deep.

Jack-in-the-Pulpit (*Arisaema triphyllum*)

Marsh-Marigold (*Caltha palustris*)

FAMILY: Buttercup (*Ranunculaceae*).

OTHER NICKNAMES: American cowslip, king-cup, May-blob, souci d'eau.

DESCRIPTION: Loose clusters of a few bright yellow flowers an inch across are borne on stems 1 to 2 ft. high; succulent heart-shaped leaves.

BLOOM PERIOD: Early spring.

OUTSTANDING FEATURE: A cheery note early in the year.

NATURAL RANGE: Labrador to Alaska; south to North Carolina, Tennessee, Iowa, and Nebraska.

CULTURE: You can make a home for this lovely harbinger of spring where your biggest downspout carries the water from the roof. In the wild it is found in swampy places, but with adequate moisture, especially in winter and spring, it can be cultivated in a low spot. Add plenty of humus when planting and mulch well. This latter practice helps conserve moisture and will also mark the spot, since the plants go dormant in summer. Hit the site with the hose from time to time in rainless periods. Early settlers ate the new greens in the spring like spinach, but nowadays with our food distribution we can easily get leafy vegetables at the store. I think it criminal for anyone now to gather marsh–marigolds for this purpose. Bloom seems best where plants get nearly full sun during early spring, then are shaded during the hot weather.

RECOMMENDED SELECTIONS: Rare white and double forms exist.

RELATED SPECIES: *C. biflora* and *C. leptosepala*, both white-flowered, are western natives. Their native haunts are subalpine, however, which means they would need wetter, cooler sites than their eastern cousin. *C. natans* from Canada and Minnesota is a real aquatic with small white to pink flowers; it is found floating on ponds.

PROPAGATION: By seed sown immediately after it ripens and kept constantly wet; by division in spring.

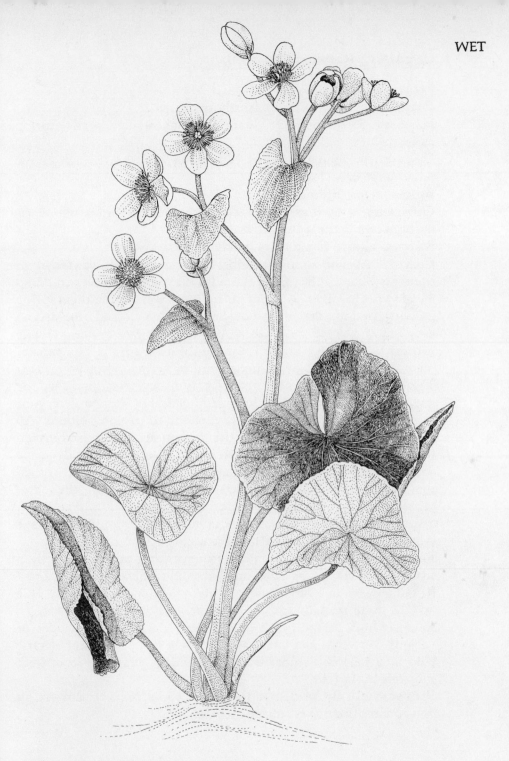

Marsh-Marigold (*Caltha palustris*)

Camas-Lily (*Camassia cusicki*)

FAMILY: Lily (*Liliaceae*).
OTHER NICKNAMES: Wild-hyacinth, quamash.
HABITAT: Rich, humusy loam; partial shade; needs spring moisture.
DESCRIPTION: Spires of starry blue flowers 3 to 4 ft. high above rather large basal leaves.
BLOOM PERIOD: Spring.
OUTSTANDING FEATURES: Dependable companion for Darwin tulips or for accent in the spring garden.
NATURAL RANGE: Oregon but hardy in northeast.
CULTURE: As with so many bulbs, camassias do not want to sit in standing water, although in the wild they are often seen in damp meadows. However, without sufficient water during their spring growing period, they will not amount to much. These are an excellent choice for spots where it is easy to give irrigation when necessary but where the soil does not remain soggy. You can aid them in the garden by adding plenty of humus when you plant. The basal leaves disappear not long after flowering, and then the site can remain quite dry. Where May is hot, try to give your camassias at least some afternoon shade to prolong bloom. All species open their flowers from the bottom up. Indians so relished the bulbs as food that wars were fought over good stands in the west. In rich soil camassias increase quite quickly by offsets. When they look crowded, wait until foliage dies down, then dig, separate, and replant immediately. Taller species should go 10 in. apart. The shorter types can go closer together, since their foliage is grassy, and they look prettiest en masse.
RELATED SPECIES: Several other western species do equally well in eastern gardens. *C. leichtlini* has both blue and white forms 2 to 3 ft. tall as well as a rare double white. *C. quamash* is usually blue and 12 to 18 in. tall, and *C. scilloides* is a much similar eastern species found as far north as southern Canada. The shades of various camassias can vary rather widely from a vibrant electric blue to a pale sky color. Bulbs are widely available from bulb suppliers in the fall.
PROPAGATION: By seed, but they take some years to flower; by division of offsets after foliage dies down.

Camas-Lily (*Camassia cusicki*)

Fraser's Sedge (*Carex fraseri*)

FAMILY: Sedge (*Cyperaceae*).
OTHER NAME: Sometimes also botanically designated as *Cymophyllus fraseri*.
HABITAT: Rich, damp, humusy soil; shade.
DESCRIPTION: Attractive evergreen straplike basal leaves; white spikes of flowers up to 2 ft. tall but usually shorter.
BLOOM PERIOD: Earliest spring.
OUTSTANDING FEATURE: Showy flowers before the garden really wakes up.
NATURAL RANGE: Virginia and West Virginia to South Carolina and Tennessee in mountains.
CULTURE: Some near relatives of this wildflower are used as foliage plants for either outdoor or indoor use, but this rather rare species excites everyone who sees it. One just does not expect such a plant so early or in a woodsy situation. Although in some instances I have hedged about how much moisture certain plants in this section on moisture–loving plants require, this one must never dry out. It should have a position with at least the filtered shade of bare trees branches in winter and good shadow the rest of the year. The soil must be rich in humus, and the plants must be in a position where they are always able to obtain moisture. Along the low banks of a stream of beside a pond are the best sites. The plants do not grow into the water, but their roots will always reach for it. If you want to try carex in a spot away from open water, make sure the soil is very rich in humus, mulch well, and be prepared to give extra water frequently if there is no rain. I can't guarantee results, but it would be a feather in your cap to succeed. This sedge is hardy at least to southeastern Pennsylvania, being a mountaineer, and it is worth trying farther north.
PROPAGATION: Division in early spring, but chancy.

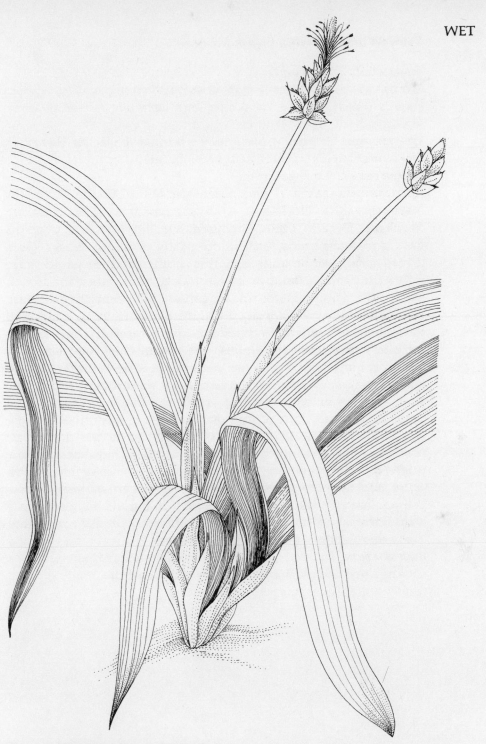

Fraser's Sedge (*Carex fraseri*)

Fairy-Wand *(Chamaelirium luteum)*

FAMILY: Lily *(Liliaceae)*.

OTHER NICKNAMES: Blazing-star, devil's-bit.

HABITAT: Rich loam on acid side with adequate moisture; some sun.

DESCRIPTION: Rosette of basal leaves with long slender cluster of tiny white flowers on erect stem 1 to 3 ft. tall.

BLOOM PERIOD: Early summer.

OUTSTANDING FEATURE: Pretty accent plant.

NATURAL RANGE: Florida to Arkansas; north to Massachusetts, New York, Ontario, Ohio, Michigan, and Illinois.

CULTURE: I have found fairy-wand mostly in sunny, grassy spots that in spring can be quite wet. It is another of those paradoxical plants that wants a damp but well-drained home, for it has a thick fleshy root that might rot. In the garden, add plenty of peatmoss when planting, mulch well, and give more shade to overcome possible dryness. Plan to add extra water if necessary, too. Under these less than ideal conditions, the bloom heights will remain on the shorter side. If you are planting in a damp area, site the fairy-wands on the edges of the wetness or on hummocks of higher land, which will keep the roots from too much moisture. This genus is dioecious, and if you do not have plants of both sexes, you will never get seed. Flowers of both sexes are attractive, however. The female ones are pure white. The males have a yellow tint from the many stamens, and often their slender spikes curve gracefully toward the top. Nurseries never sex them, so you will just have to take your chances. If you put in enough original plants, the law of averages is in your favor. I do not know how hardy this plant is beyond its natural range.

PROPAGATION: By seed sown in situ as soon as it is ripe (seed does not keep well and must not dry out); division of rhizomatous roots when dormant, but this is chancy.

Fairy-Wand (*Chamaelirium luteum*)

White Turtle-Head (*Chelone glabra*)

FAMILY: Snapdragon (*Scrophulariaceae*).

OTHER NICKNAMES: Snake-head, balmony.

HABITAT: Moist, humusy soil; nearly full sun.

DESCRIPTION: Small, narrow clusters of white flowers, sometimes tinged pink, which resemble snapdragons along stalks 2 to 4 ft. high.

BLOOM PERIOD: Late summer into fall.

OUTSTANDING FEATURE: A good late-blooming perennial.

NATURAL RANGE: Newfoundland to Ontario and Minnesota; south to Georgia, Alabama, and Missouri.

CULTURE: Chelone can be tamed for the garden if you plant it in a low spot where it is easy to add water in drought, but it definitely will not grow in dry areas or where there is too much competition from tree roots. Use plenty of peat moss when planting and mulch well to keep the moisture in. I have a patch in the garden in rather clayey soil where water collects in hard rain but never stands. This colony is increasing nicely, so must be happy. A rabbit taught me an interesting lesson: when spring growth has reached about 6 inches, nip off the chelone's tender tips. This produces fine, bushy, branching plants, less tall and much more floriferous. In wetter spots, chelone easily reaches 3 ft., but the stems are sturdy and need no staking. It will take a little shade, but blooms best with lots of sun. Unfortunately, deer like it, too. From a side view it is quite eerie how much the individual flower does resemble a turtle with its mouth open.

RELATED SPECIES: *C. lyoni* is a pink-flowered species from the southern mountains that is hardy in northern states, particularly if given a moist enough site. Bloom begins a bit later than in the white. I have grown it in clay soil that, while moist, is not wet in summer. Under these conditions it has flowered well but remained under 15 in. Along streams it easily reaches 3 ft. Red turtle-head (*C. obliqua*) from the southern swamps has flowers closer to purple, grows at least as tall as *C. glabra*, and reputedly is hardy north of Philadelphia.

PROPAGATION: By seed; by division in spring.

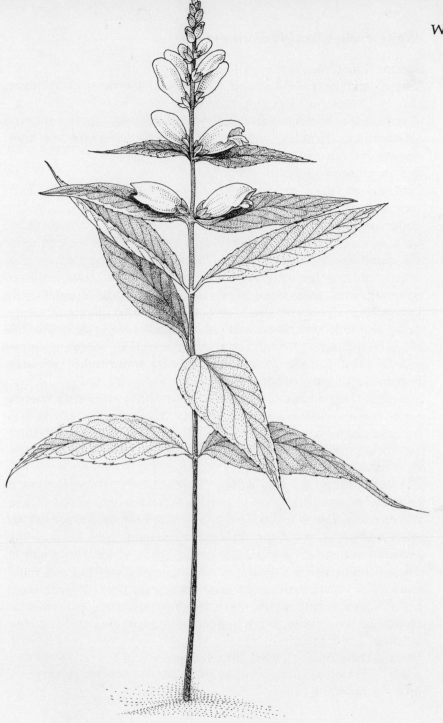

White Turtle-Head (*Chelone glabra*)

White Trout-Lily (*Erythronium albidum*)

FAMILY: Lily (*Liliaceae*).

OTHER NICKNAMES: White adder's-tongue, dogtooth-violet, fawn lily.

HABITAT: Moist, rich, neutral soil; summer shade.

DESCRIPTION: Nodding white solitary bells a few inches high; leaves sometimes mottled, nearly flat on ground.

BLOOM PERIOD: Spring.

NATURAL RANGE: Ontario to Minnesota; south to Georgia, Kentucky, Missouri, and Oklahoma.

CULTURE: Sometimes tinged violet, these trout-lilies are more apt to bloom in gardens than their better-known yellow eastern sister (*E. americanum*). Since this midwestern species prefers neutral soil, I mulch mine with marble chips. This also prevents inadvertent disturbance, since all erythronium foliage disappears by summertime. This one also grows in moist bottomlands. Plant the bulbs only 3 to 4 in. deep in fall and place a stone underneath; this often encourages bloom. The narrow-leaved *E. mesachoreum* is considered a lavender form of *albidum* by some and is reputedly even easier to grow in humusy garden soil.

RECOMMENDED HYBRIDS AND SELECTIONS: Improved and selected western trout-lilies are even better bets for gardens and take drier soil, too. Many produce more than one flower per stem. Good for garden culture are Kondo and Pagoda (yellow), White Beauty, Rose Beauty.

RELATED SPECIES: *E. americanum* is very hardy and will grow in half-shaded woodland that is very wet, but it always produces far more leaves than flowers. It prefers soil on the acid side. Try the stone technique to encourage flowers instead of new bulbs. Some western species are quite easy to flower in woodland gardens. They want humusy soil and get along nicely without too much wet; most prefer a dry summer. They, too, may have multiple flowers per stem. Look for *grandiflorum* and *tuolumnensis* (yellow), *revolutum* (white), *hendersoni* (purple), *californicum* (cream).

PROPAGATION: All by seed, but it takes some years before they reach blooming size. Propagate eastern species (except *E. mesachoreum*) by offsets.

White Trout-Lily (*Erythronium albidum*)

Bottle Gentian (*Gentiana andrewsi*)

FAMILY: Gentian (*Gentianaceae*).
OTHER NICKNAMES: Blind, closed, or fringe-tip gentian.
HABITAT: Moist, slightly acid soil; part shade.
DESCRIPTION: Clusters of small, balloon-shaped violet–blue flowers in axils of upper leaves; 1 to 2 ft. high.
BLOOM PERIOD: Fall.
OUTSTANDING FEATURE: Late-flowering source of blue.
NATURAL RANGE: Quebec to Manitoba and Saskatchewan; south to Georgia and Arkansas.
CULTURE: Yes, most gentians are difficult to grow, but this hardy native is not, particularly under the right conditions. Soil should have plenty of humus and never dry out (although it should never be mucky wet either). A good mulch keeps the roots cool. At least in southerly latitudes it should also get summer afternoon shade. Good air circulation is another suggested precaution, and protection from slugs wise. The flowers never open, hence the various nicknames. While it is never as striking as some of the open gentians, the adaptability of this one to cultivation is a big plus. When grown in some quantity, a colony is really quite beautiful. Color is variable with some plants even being pure white, but usually flowers are more purple than blue. This is a good choice for a damp, low spot in half–shade.
RELATED SPECIES: *G. clausa* is quite similar but harder to tame. *G. linearis* (narrow-leaved) has slenderer flowers, too; it flowers earlier but demands a much more acid soil. Two other closed gentians are sometimes sold. *G. decora* (Allegheny Mountain) is said to be the last gentian to bloom, while *G. saponaria* (soap-wort) is the first to come into flower. Both are very hardy, so if you can get a good colony of *G. andrewsi* going, add these other two to prolong your color. Two western species are suggested for neutral to slightly acid, moist soil with plenty of humus and some shade. *G. calycosa* is up to 10 in. high and has a few bell-shaped blue flowers, often streaked green. *G. oregana* may go to 2 ft., has blue open flowers. I would mulch both well in eastern gardens, and I do not know how hardy they are.
PROPAGATION: By seed; by division in spring.

Bottle Gentian (*Gentiana andrewsi*)

Rose-Mallow (*Hibiscus palustris*)

FAMILY: Mallow (*Malvaceae*).
OTHER NICKNAMES: Mallow-rose, sea-hollyhock.
HABITAT: Damp, not too rich soil; full sun.
DESCRIPTION: Hollyhocklike flowers 4 or 5 in. across in pink, purple, or white with a red eye; plants 3 to 8 ft. high; big, rather coarse leaves.
BLOOM PERIOD: Most of summer.
OUTSTANDING FEATURE: Good summer color for wet places.
NATURAL RANGE: Coastal Massachusetts to North Carolina; inland New York to Ontario, west around Great Lakes.
CULTURE: In garden soil, this flamboyant native will have smaller flowers on shorter stalks. If you water it deeply during the summer, there is no reason why you cannot grow it that way, but most gardeners prefer to use one of the many fine hybrids instead. All types make big clumps in time, so do allow enough room. The plants are late in showing growth in the spring, and where winters are severe a light mulch is recommended for both species and hybrids. Since this species thrives in a wet spot, it is ideal for swampy places where not much else will do well. Because it is apparently not affected by salt, it is also an excellent choice for low spots along highways where residues from winter road–clearing are apt to collect. Garden clubs trying to beautify such ugly areas would do well to consider this species.
RECOMMENDED HYBRIDS: Our hardy native hibiscus have been crossed with more tropical species to develop some magnificent hybrids. They are offered in color selections from crimson through the pinks to white and can have blossoms a foot in diameter; the plants are usually under 4 ft. Southern Belle is a red-eyed hybrid often blooming the first year from seed. It won All-America Selection in 1971 and is now offered in separate colors.
RELATED SPECIES: *H. moscheutos* (wild-cotton) is a more southerly species with creamy white petals and a dark red eye. It has slightly less coarse foliage and has also been used in hybridizing.
PROPAGATION: By seed, but start early in the house; by division in spring after shoots show.

Rose-Mallow (*Hibiscus palustris*)

Bluets (*Houstonia caerulea*)

FAMILY: Madder (*Rubiaceae*).
NICKNAMES: Quaker-ladies, angel-eyes, innocence.
HABITAT: Somewhat acid soil that does not get too dry; sun.
DESCRIPTION: Tiny blue flowers (or more rarely, white) with a yellow eye on 4-in. stems above basal rosette of foliage.
BLOOM PERIOD: Most of spring.
OUTSTANDING FEATURE: Dainty diminutive for edging or rock garden.
NATURAL RANGE: Nova Scotia to Ontario and Wisconsin; south to Georgia, Alabama, and Missouri.
CULTURE: Authorities seem to differ on how much moisture this plant wants. Perhaps in the northern part of its range it does not require as much. I only know that plants in a section of my garden where the soil seldom dries out have proved much longer-lived than those in a better-drained spot. Add plenty of peat moss when planting to increase the sponginess of the soil and its acidity. My bluets take partial shade without harm, but sun is preferred. A mulch helps keep the roots cooler, for in the wild, bluets are usually found growing right in grass, a natural mulch. Often a meadow will literally turn blue when the bluets are at their height. It is a strange commentary on life that rock gardeners go to all sorts of extremes to locate tiny plants from odd corners of the world and often forget this darling. Perhaps they are put off by its commonness in grassy fields, but bluets are not always easy to establish in the garden. They are another delight for which one must kneel to enjoy completely—not a bad way to spend a few moments on a lovely spring day.
RELATED SPECIES: *H. serpyllifolia* (thyme-leaved or creeping bluets) is an even tinier plant, but the flowers are often longer-stemmed. It takes quite moist ground, and because of its creeping tendencies makes a pretty groundcover for such spots. It, too, will take some shade and is sometimes used in terrariums. *H. purpurea* (mountain bluets) has clusters of flowers from 4 to 18 in. high, and color ranges from nearly white to pale purple. I would not expect either of these species to be as hardy as common bluets.
PROPAGATION: By seed; by division in spring.

Bluets (*Houstonia caerulea*)

Cardinal-Flower (*Lobelia cardinalis*)

FAMILY: Lobelia (*Lobeliaceae*).
OTHER NICKNAMES: Red lobelia, Indian-pink, red-birds.
HABITAT: Moist but well-drained loam on acid side; part shade.
DESCRIPTION: Brilliant red flowers on a long, narrow inflorescence from 2 to 4 ft. tall; basal foliage evergreen where winter is not too harsh.
BLOOM PERIOD: Late summer.
OUTSTANDING FEATURES: Wonderful accent for late summer garden and very attractive to hummingbirds.
NATURAL RANGE: New Brunswick to Ontario; south to Florida and Texas.
CULTURE: In the wild cardinal-flower is found along stream banks and in wettish places, but it can be adapted to the garden. Add plenty of peat moss when planting and mulch well to keep the soil cool and moist. A slight depression where it is easy to add extra moisture in times of drought makes your task easier, but often the plants self–sow in much drier sites than planned. Winter kill is often serious where there is not sufficient moisture in the soil; a good mulch combats this. Many gardeners separate and replant the clusters of new basal rosettes in the fall after bloom is over, but this can be a tricky proposition where frost comes early. Probably the best idea is to sow seed around the mother plants each year in the late fall so that vigorous new plants are constantly coming. The seed is very fine. Some gardeners feel flower stalks should be removed before the seed matures to cut drain on the mother plant. I always let at least one stalk go to seed. Where summers are sunny and hot, give your cardinal–flowers some filtered afternoon shade or the flowers will not be as brilliant in color. This precaution also assures soil that is more moist.
RECOMMENDED SELECTIONS AND HYBRIDS: There is a pure white form sometimes offered. Hybrids between this red lobelia and its blue sister (see following description) also exist but are not yet in commerce. Those I have seen are in lavender shades, but I keep hoping one will come along in a lovely pink.
PROPAGATION: By seed; by offsets; by stem cuttings.

Cardinal-Flower (*Lobelia cardinalis*)

Great Blue Lobelia (*Lobelia siphilitica*)

FAMILY: Lobelia (*Lobeliaceae*).
OTHER NICKNAME: Blue cardinal-flower.
HABITAT: Moist rich soil; sun or partial shade.
DESCRIPTION: Dense spikes of small blue flowers on stout stems 1 to 3 ft. high; basal foliage evergreen where winters are not too harsh.
BLOOM PERIOD: Late summer into fall.
OUTSTANDING FEATURES: Very easy plant for wet spots and a welcome source of late blue.
NATURAL RANGE: Maine to Minnesota and South Dakota; south to Virginia, Louisiana, and Texas.
CULTURE: Much less difficult to keep in the garden than its red counterpart, the blue lobelia can even become a bit of a weed because it self–sows freely. It is shallow-rooted, however, so easy to remove where not wanted. In one packet of seed there is likely to be great variation in hue, all the way from dark, almost navy, to a pale sky color. White variants are not uncommon, and often you will have some of them present, too. If you have room for a good-sized colony in a wet spot, you will find that various plants bloom at different times, thus extending flowering from July to frost. Peat moss added when planting and some mulch are helpful where the soil is drier, but I have truly had little trouble in growing this lobelia in a variety of locations. Where the soil is damp, it does nicely in full sun, but a touch of shade does not seem to affect flowering. Never let the plants get too dry in warm weather. Unfortunately, deer relish the spikes of both lobelias, and this can spoil any flowering where they are a problem.
RECOMMENDED SELECTIONS AND HYBRIDS: If you want a colony of the white form, you will annually have to weed out blue seedlings as they come into bloom because the progeny do not all breed true. For word on hybrids, look to the cardinal-flower discussion just preceding.
PROPAGATION: By seed; by division in spring.

Great Blue Lobelia (*Lobelia siphilitica*)

Barbara's-Buttons (*Marshallia grandiflora*)

FAMILY: Daisy (*Compositae*).
HABITAT: Moist, humusy soil; half shade.
DESCRIPTION: Lavender daisies, about an inch across, with blue anthers on 1– to 2–ft. stems; basal foliage evergreen in my garden.
BLOOM PERIOD: Late spring into summer.
OUTSTANDING FEATURES: A rare, beautiful daisy.
NATURAL RANGE: Pennsylvania to Kentucky; south to North Carolina.
CULTURE: How sad that hardly any gardeners even know of the existence of this lovely native, much less where to obtain it. Most of the other species have a much more southerly range, but this grows wild at least as far north as the Alleghenies below Pittsburgh, which is pretty rugged country. I am told that in a really moist situation marshallia is a much better grower and quickly makes fine colonies. Around here I have seen it seeding itself in a half-shady garden that is moist woodland rather than any kind of bog. I would suggest it as a companion plant for primroses, since it seems to like the same situation. If you can locate a source of seed or plants, do try it in the garden with humusy soil and some shade. Locate it in a slight depression so you can add extra water in hot, dry weather. And of course if you have a low damp spot, put some there, too. Perhaps together we can convince dealers to add this to their lists so others may enjoy a real woodland daisy. What it needs is a press agent, I guess. From what I have read it was once more popular than now for garden use, and I suspect it may be doubtfully hardy in the far north. Perhaps at one time the forms offered were of the more southerly species. Pink and white forms have been reported, but I have never seen them. The genus is named, incidentally, not for the marsh where it likes to grow, but for Humphrey Marshall, an early American botanist.
PROPAGATION: By seed; by division in spring.

Barbara's-Buttons (*Marshallia grandiflora*)

Virginia Bluebell (*Mertensia virginica*)

FAMILY: Borage (*Boraginaceae*).
OTHER NICKNAMES: Virginia-cowslip, Roanoke-bells.
HABITAT: Rich loam with adequate spring moisture; sun to part shade.
DESCRIPTION: Arching stems 1 to 3 ft. high bear clusters of pink buds that open to small blue bells.
BLOOM PERIOD: Spring.
OUTSTANDING FEATURE: Excellent for moist bottomlands.
NATURAL RANGE: Ontario to Minnesota; south to South Carolina, Alabama, Arkansas, and Kansas.
CULTURE: These dainty bluebells bloom much better in northern regions if they have nearly full sun during the early spring months. A site under late-leafing deciduous trees or trees that give high filtered shade is best. The crucial factor for lush fountains of blossom is adequate spring moisture. Add humus to the soil when planting, mulch well, and use the hose if spring is dry. I have for some years tended a great plantation of these plants. It is sometimes under water for a few days during spring floods, and the tubers have had great quantities of silt dumped upon them of late. They continue to bloom beautifully since we cleared away the surrounding brush, so the plants get good spring sunshine. Later shade and even some summer dryness does not matter, since the plants complete their growing cycle and die down by the end of June. This early withering away makes them a bit difficult to site in the garden, but their springtime show is so ethereal it is worth a bit of extra trouble. Plant something in the area to take over after the mertensia dies down. Ferns are good. Mature mertensia tubers are best treated like bulbs and planted 1 to 2 in. deep in fall, when they are widely offered. Eventually, in the right spot, a single tuber makes a large clump. Large roots can be divided during dormancy, but it is wiser to encourage self-sowing to increase a stand.
RECOMMENDED SELECTIONS: A pure white form is sometimes available. There is also a pink, but I have never seen it listed.
RELATED SPECIES: Other mertensias, some quite dwarf, are found across the country, but I prefer the eastern one for garden decoration. Don't let that discourage you from trying your local species.
PROPAGATION: By seed; by division as foliage dies down.

Virginia Bluebell (*Mertensia virginica*)

American Lotus (*Nelumbo pentapetala*)

FAMILY: Waterlily (*Nymphaeaceae*).
OTHER NICKNAMES: Yellow lotus, water chinquapin, nelumbium.
Sometimes also botanically designated as *N. lutea.*
HABITAT: Ponds and slowly moving streams; sun.
DESCRIPTION: Large pale yellow flowers, plate-sized leaves as much as 2 ft. across, both borne high above the water.
BLOOM PERIOD: Summer.
OUTSTANDING FEATURE: Very hardy decorative for water garden.
NATURAL RANGE: Ontario to Minnesota and Iowa; south to Florida, Louisiana and Texas.
CULTURE: Since this aquatic plant does well in shallow water, it can even be adapted to small garden pools, but these should be at least 2 ft. deep. You need 3 or 4 in. of water above the top of the plant container. Nelumbo spreads rapidly by creeping roots. When grown in containers, the roots must be separated every few seasons because bloom is best if plants are not too crowded. A clayey soil is recommended. When preparing a tub planting, mix some well-rotted cow manure or bulb fertilizer in soil before planting. Indians used both fleshy roots and seeds for food. Muskrats also consider them a delicacy. Chicken–wire baskets can be made to protect the tubers somewhat. In a pond, plant the first few roots in wire-covered containers, and you can usually count on at least a few plants free from the rats. Their dining keeps a free-growing stand from getting too crowded. The large pyramidal lotus seedpods are much sought by arrangers of dried materials. Plants are mostly available from dealers in aquatic supplies. They usually sell wooden tubs for planting also. A rock is usually placed on newly planted roots either in pond or in container, but be careful it does not lay atop the brittle new growing point. This lotus can be wintered in situ as long as roots are below the ice. See under *Nymphaea odorata* for more tips.
PROPAGATION: By seed. File the large ripe seeds first, then wrap in a ball of clay and drop in shallow water; or file through the shell, then soak in tepid water two days, after which sow in sand that must be kept warm and wet until seeds sprout. Plant seedlings in small boxes and submerge on edge of sunny pool until plants grow larger and are ready to go into deeper water. Division of thick tuberous roots is recommended in fall.

American Lotus (*Nelumbo pentapetala*)

Spatterdock (*Nuphar advena*)

FAMILY: Waterlily (*Nymphaeaceae*).
OTHER NICKNAMES: Cow-lily, yellow pond-lily.
HABITAT: Ponds or slow streams where water is at least 2 ft. deep; sun.
DESCRIPTION: Globe-shaped yellow flowers 2 to 3 in. across and large oval leaves usually float on water but sometimes are slightly above it.
BLOOM PERIOD: All summer.
OUTSTANDING FEATURE: Adds interest to large water area.
NATURAL RANGE: Massachusetts to Wisconsin and Nebraska; south to Florida and Texas.
CULTURE: A vigorous spreader by large creeping roots, nuphar is also not decorative enough to cultivate in any small body of water. For a large pond, however, it has some merit because of the very long blooming period. The globe flowers never open entirely, and the seed capsule is borne above water. To get a planting started, anchor roots, available usually from aquatic suppliers, in the lake or stream bottom with a rock in at least 2 ft. of water during spring.
RELATED SPECIES: *N. saggitifolium* has long, narrow arrow-shaped leaves and is less hardy. *N. microphyllum* has smaller leaves and flowers and grows as far north as Canada. It would be a far wiser choice for a pond of restricted dimensions, but frankly either the lotus or the true waterlily of this section are far superior as garden decoratives.
PROPAGATION: By seed as for lotus; by division of roots in spring.

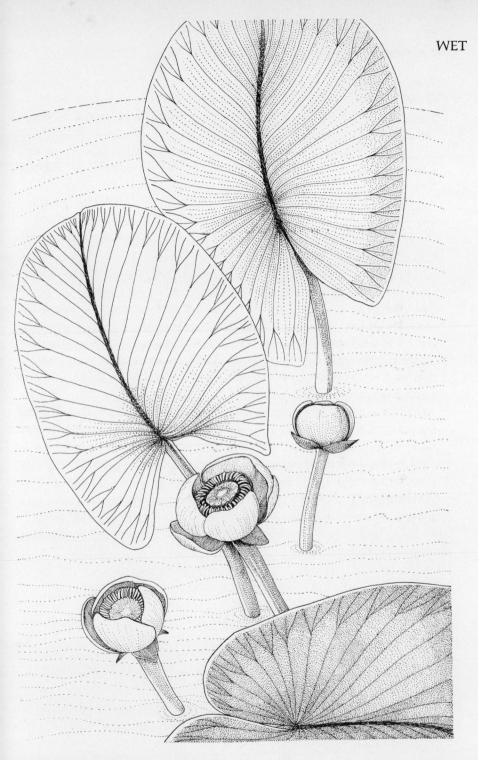

Spatterdock (*Nuphar advena*)

Fragrant Waterlily (*Nymphaea odorata*)

FAMILY: Waterlily (*Nymphaeaceae*).

OTHER NICKNAME: Hardy waterlily.

HABITAT: Warm, shallow ponds and sluggish streams; sun.

DESCRIPTION: White or pink fragrant double flowers 2 to 4 in. across and round leaves 2 to 10 in. across, both floating.

BLOOM PERIOD: Summer.

OUTSTANDING FEATURES: Very hardy, fragrant, day-blooming.

NATURAL RANGE: Newfoundland to Manitoba; south to Florida and Texas.

CULTURE: This lovely waterlily is classified as a miniature by aquatic experts. As such it can be grown in a 6-in. flower pot submerged in a small pool. Mix a handful of bulb or waterlily fertilizer with soil on clayey side, saturate with water, then plant the root so it is covered to the crown. Three Springs Fisheries suggests adding an inch of sand at the top to prevent any resident fish from roiling the surface of the planter. The pot is then gently lowered into the water and propped at a proper depth. A mature plant needs at least 12 in. of water above the pot so the leaves can float on the water surface. In starting a plant, you may find it best to put a rock or bricks under the pot so it is only a few inches below the water level until growth begins; then lower pot later. If your pool is deep enough so the roots in the pot can winter below the ice line, you can lower the pot to the bottom and leave it there when cold weather arrives. With a shallower pool, store containers in a cool (not freezing) spot and keep soil moist. Bring out again when the ice breaks up in spring. In a natural pond anchor the roots with a stone when planting initially. See under nelumbo for muskrat protection.

RECOMMENDED HYBRIDS: Our hardy American waterlilies have been bred with the exotic Asian species to produce hybrids in many colors and sizes. Consult a specialist's catalog.

RELATED SPECIES: *N. tetragona* is a very hardy tiny copy useful in small cold pools. *N. tuberosa* is also very hardy but a rapid root spreader and larger in every way than the others. *N. mexicana* is hardy into New England if not frozen and bears odorless yellow blooms.

PROPAGATION: Fleshy fruits form under water and seed must be kept wet at all times; tubers or roots may be separated carefully in spring when they become crowded.

Fragrant Waterlily (*Nymphaea odorata*)

American Burnet (*Sanguisorba canadensis*)

FAMILY: Rose (*Rosaceae*).

OTHER NICKNAMES: Great burnet, herbe à pisser.

HABITAT: Marshes and wet spots in acid soil; sun but likes a cool climate.

DESCRIPTION: Small white flowers in dense spikes as long as 6 in. at top of sturdy stems 3 to 6 ft. high; foliage pinnately compound.

BLOOM PERIOD: Late summer into early autumn.

OUTSTANDING FEATURE: Late season color for the water garden.

NATURAL RANGE: Labrador to Michigan; south to Newfoundland, New Jersey, Delaware, and in the mountains to Georgia, Ohio, Indiana, and Illinois.

CULTURE: You will not find it easy to locate a start of this plant or even the seed itself; but if you have a wet garden, it is well worth a prolonged search. Burnet spreads into stately patches along the banks of streams and in wet places. English gardeners report it growing in dampish garden situations, but I would doubt this possible in warmer climates. You will note that it is a plant of the north. The farther south you live, the more important a really wet environment becomes. Some afternoon shade may be necessary, too, to keep it cool. Use acid sphagnum peat liberally when planting. You should know that this is not the same as *S. officinalis*, the European burnet used as a salad herb and to flavor wine.

PROPAGATION: By seeds kept damp in a sandy peat medium; by division of roots in spring.

American Burnet (*Sanguisorba canadensis*)

Lizard-Tail (*Saururus cernuus*)

FAMILY: Lizard-tail (*Sauruaceae*).

OTHER NICKNAMES: Water-dragon, swamp-lily.

HABITAT: Mucky verges of ponds, streams, and swamps; mostly shade.

DESCRIPTION: Dense, graceful terminal spikes of fragrant white flowers borne 2 to 5 ft. high; large heart–shaped leaves.

BLOOM PERIOD: Summer.

OUTSTANDING FEATURES: Delicious vanilla fragrance of flowers; ability to grow where it is wet all the time.

NATURAL RANGE: Quebec and Ontario to Michigan; south to Florida and Texas.

CULTURE: Think carefully about planting this marsh–lover beside a tiny pool or a little brook. This native is a real spreader and would rapidly take over, but for a larger area few plants could be more beautiful, especially at night when the white flowers come into their own under the moonlight. The tapering white spires tend to droop over much like a shepherd's crook, and the sweet perfume is delicious. I would not suggest this plant for other than a really wet place. Along waterways the spreading rootstocks can help hold banks in, for they are far–reaching. The most common names are rather unkind, referring to the curve of the spikes. Swamp–lily is a bit of a misnomer, however, because there is no resemblance to a lily. The only close relative of this American is an Asiatic species. (If you delve very deeply into the taxonomy and geographical distribution of plants, you will be surprised to see how many North American natives have counterparts in Japan, Manchuria, and Korea. Dicentra and jeffersonia are two more that come quickly to mind. It all has something to do with continental drift. The most surprising thing is that while the Japanese dicentra differs rather greatly from our types, the American and Asian saururus and jeffersonia are not all that unalike.)

PROPAGATION: By seed; by division in spring.

Lizard-Tail (*Saururus cernuus*)

Blue-Eyed-Grass (*Sisyrinchium angustifolium*)

FAMILY: Iris (*Iridaceae*).
OTHER NICKNAMES: Satin-flower, rush-lily.
HABITAT: Moist spots preferred, but very adaptable; sun or partial shade.
DESCRIPTION: Little blue–violet stars with a golden eye above tufts of clean foliage; seldom 1 ft. high.
BLOOM PERIOD: Spring into summer.
OUTSTANDING FEATURES: A dainty thing that takes care of itself and blooms its heart out almost anywhere.
NATURAL RANGE: Newfoundland to Ontario; south to Florida and Texas.
CULTURE: In the wild one is most apt to find this tiny darling in low spots where rain collects, but I have grown it in extremely dry spots almost as well. Bloom is best with sun, but again it does quite well in part shade, too. Why then is it not more planted? I suppose because it just is not spectacular. The flowers are seldom even an inch across, and they last only part of a day. But if the round seed heads are quickly removed, blue–eyed–grass continues to flower for a long time. Planted in quantity, it makes a lovely mass of color for the morning gardener. Since many plants will not prosper in damp spots, this is a good choice to hold the soil there. It does self–sow prodigiously, but the seedlings are easy to weed out if they get out of bounds. The foliage, which resembles a thin iris, is evergreen where winters are not too harsh.
RELATED SPECIES: Several other sisyrinchiums are native to the east, and the differences are negligible. The white form of *S. mucronatum*, however, is a real jewel. *S. californicum* from the west coast has little yellow flowers, wants a sunny, moist site, but is not nearly as hardy. *S. douglasi* (*S. grandiflorum*) from the northwest is the real star of the family and is offered by several western suppliers. Its spring flowers are at least three times as large as the eastern species, usually pink to purple but sometimes also available in selected white or orchid forms. It is quite hardy, being found even in Idaho, and dedicated rock gardeners already appreciate its beauty. Known as grass widows, *S. douglasi* wants a sunny, well–drained spot. It disappears after flowering and needs as dry a summer and fall as possible.
PROPAGATION: By seed; by division almost any time.

Blue-Eyed-Grass (*Sisyrinchium angustifolium*)

Tall Meadow-Rue (*Thalictrum polygamum*)

FAMILY: Buttercup (*Ranunculaceae*).

OTHER NICKNAMES: Muskrat-weed, musquash-weed, musketweed.

HABITAT: Moist, rich loam; sun or partial shade.

DESCRIPTION: Large erect clusters of fluffy white bloom on stout, branched stalks 3 to 10 ft. tall; foliage very dainty.

BLOOM PERIOD: Summer.

OUTSTANDING FEATURES: Tall, graceful summer accent.

NATURAL RANGE: Newfoundland to Ontario; south to Georgia and Tennessee.

CULTURE: The hotter your summers, the more you need to make sure this meadow–rue has sufficient moisture and some afternoon shade. I have grown it successfully for many years in a low spot where the soil is more clay than humus and where it gets extra water only when it rains. Under these less friendly conditions, it seldom tops 5 ft. and has not increased greatly, but bloom is always good. My plants have never needed any staking. The flowers, although not long–lasting when cut, are lovely in bouquets. I would certainly not hesitate to plant it at the back of any garden, but it also revels in swampy spots.

RELATED SPECIES: *T. dioicum* (early meadow–rue) is quite a different kind of plant, blooming in the spring. Its rather insignificant drooping yellowish flowers have reddish purple tints. Given some early spring sun, it will flourish where there is deep summer shade and where the soil eventually gets quite dry. The dainty compound foliage makes a 2–ft. bush, seems to have no enemies, and remains a lovely silvery green even in drought years. It is a nice accent plant for shade, but be forewarned that the creeping roots travel. I rip out the extras in the spring whenever they get out of bounds. *T. occidentale* is a rather similar westerner, wanting moist open woods. *T. polycarpum* is the tall meadow–rue of the west coast and much like its white–flowered eastern sister. *T. venulosum* from the Rockies has pale green flowers, makes a mound 18 in. high, and takes a dry sunny site. All the thalictrums are delightful as much for their foliage as the flowers. There are several other easterners which are seldom offered commercially; none has more to offer than those described here.

PROPAGATION: By seed; by division in early spring.

Tall Meadow-Rue (*Thalictrum polygamum*)

Appendix:
Seed and Plant Suppliers

Mostly Seed

W. Atlee Burpee Co.
300 Park Ave.
Warminster,
Pennsylvania 18974

*Leslie's Wild Flower Nursery (25¢)
30 Summer St.
Methuen, Massachusetts 01844

*Far North Gardens (35¢)
15621 Auburndale Ave.
Livonia, Michigan 48154

*Midwest Wildflowers (25¢)
Box 64
Rockton, Illinois 61072

*J. L. Hudson (50¢)
P.O. Box 1058
Redwood City,
California 94064

Northplan Seed Producers
P.O. Box 9107
Moscow, Idaho 83843

*Denotes especially varied native lists

Please note charges where indicated for catalogs

*George W. Park Seed Co.
P.O. Box 31
Greenwood,
South Carolina 29647

Prairie Gem Ranch
Smithwick, South Dakota 57782

*Clyde Robin Seed Co. ($1)
Box 2855
Castro Valley, California 94546

Thompson & Morgan, Inc.
P.O. Box 24
401 Kennedy Blvd.
Somerdale, New Jersey 08083

*Windrift Prairie Shop (25¢)
R.D. 2
Oregon, Illinois 61061

Mostly Aquatics

Paradise Gardens ($1)
Bedford and May Sts.
Whitman, Massachusetts 02382

Slocum Water Gardens
1101 Cypress Gardens Rd.
Winter Haven, Florida 33880

*Three Springs Fisheries ($1)
1606 Hort Rd.
Lilypons, Maryland 21717

William Tricker, Inc. (25¢)
Box 398, Dept. J-9
Saddle River, New Jersey 07458

Wildlife Nurseries
P.O. Box 2724
Oshkosh, Wisconsin 54901

Mostly Plants

Arthur Eames Allgrove (50¢)
North Wilmington,
Massachusetts 01887

Alpenglow Gardens (50¢)
13328 King George Hwy.
Surrey, British Columbia

*Alpines West Gardens & Nursery
Rt. #2, Box 259
Spokane, Washington 99207

Ashby's Garden Centre
R. R. 2
Cameron, Ontario
Canada KOM 1GO

Vernon Barnes & Son Nursery
P.O. Box 250-L
McMinnville, Tennessee 37110

*Beersheba Wildflower Gardens
Beersheba Springs,
Tennessee 37305

Blackthorne Gardens ($1)
48 Quincy St.
Holbrook, Massachusetts 02343

Bluestone Perennials, Inc.
3500 Jackson St.
Mentor, Ohio 44060

*Conley's Garden Center (35¢)
Boothbay Harbor, Maine 04538

C. A. Cruikshank Ltd.
1015 Mount Pleasant Rd.
Toronto, Ontario
Canada M4P 2MI

*Ferndale Nursery and
Greenhouse (13¢)
P.O. Box 218
Askov, Minnesota 55704

Fernhill Farm
Rt. 3, Box 191
Greenville, Alabama 36037

*Garden Place
6780 Heisley Rd.
Mentor, Ohio 44060

*Gardens of the Blue Ridge
P.O. Box 10
Pineola, North Carolina 28662

*Griffey's Nursery
Rt: 3, B 17A
Madison Cty, Marshall,
North Carolina 28753

Gurney Seed & Nursery Co.
Yankton, South Dakota 57078

Ruth Hardy
Wildflower and Fern Nursery
Falls Village, Connecticut 06031

*Henderson's Botanical Gardens
Rt. 6
Greensburg, Indiana 47240

Ruth Tate Hi Mt. Nursery (13¢)
Rt. 1, Box 61
Seligman, Missouri 65745

*International Growers
Exchange ($3)
P.O. Box 397
Farmington, Michigan 48024

*Jamieson Valley Gardens ($1)
Jamieson Rd., Rt. 3
Spokane, Washington 99203

*Lamb Nurseries
E. 101 Sharp Ave.
Spokane, Washington 99202

*Lounsberry Gardens (25¢)
P.O. Box 135
Oakford, Illinois 62673

Mincemoyer Nursery (25¢)
Rt. 526
Jackson, New Jersey 08527

Miniature Gardens ($1)
Box 757
Stony Plain, Alberta
Canada TOE 2GO

Charles H. Mueller Bulbs
River Rd.
New Hope, Pennsylvania 18938

*Orchid Gardens (35¢)
Rt. 1, Box 245
Grand Rapids, Minnesota 55744

Palette Gardens (50¢)
26 W. Zion Hill Rd., Rt. 309
Quakertown, Pennsylvania 18951

*Radford H. Palmer
R.F.D. No. 1
Durham, New Hampshire 03824

*Putney Nursery
Putney, Vermont 05346

Rakestraw's Perennial
Gardens (50¢)
G-3094 S. Term St.
Burton, Michigan 48529

Savage Gardens
P.O. Box 163
McMinnville, Tennessee 37110

John Scheepers, Inc.
63 Wall St.
New York, New York 10005

*Shop in the Sierra ($1)
Box 1
Midpines, California 95345

*Siskiyou Rare Plant Nursery (50¢)
522 Franquette St.
Medford, Oregon 97501

Van Bourgondien Bros.
P.O. Box A
245 Farmingdale Rd., Rt. 109
Babylon, New York 11702

*Vick's Wildgardens, Inc. (25¢)
Conshohocken State Rd., Box 115
Gladwyne, Pennsylvania 19035

*Wayside Gardens ($1)
Hodges, South Carolina 29695

*The Wild Garden ($1)
Box 487
Bothell, Washington 98011

*Woodland Acres Nursery (15¢)
Crivitz, Wisconsin 54114

*Woodstream Nursery (25¢)
Box 510
Jackson, New Jersey 08527

Bibliography

Bibliography

Aiken, George D. *Pioneering with Wildflowers*. Englewood Cliffs, N.J.: Prentice-Hall, 1968.

Bailey, L. H. *Manual of Cultivated Plants*. New York: Macmillan, 1968.

Cumming, Roderick W., and Robert E. Lee, *Contemporary Perennials*. New York: Macmillan, 1960.

Fernald, M. L. *Gray's Manual of Botany*, 8th ed. New York: American Book Co., 1950.

Grimm, William C. *Recognizing Flowering Wild Plants*. Harrisburg: Stackpole Books, 1968 (paperback edition, New York: Hawthorn Books, 1974).

Haskin, Leslie L. *Wild Flowers of the Pacific Coast*. Portland, Ore.: Metropolitan Press, 1934.

Henderson, Jan. *Flowers of the Parks*. Longmire, Wash.: Mount Rainier Natural History Association, 1972.

Kolaga, Walter A. *All about Rock Gardens and Plants*. Garden City, N.Y.: Doubleday, 1966.

Miles, Bebe. *Bluebells & Bittersweet: Gardening with Native American Plants*. New York: Van Nostrand Reinhold Co., 1970.

_____. *The Wonderful World of Bulbs*. New York: D. Van Nostrand Co., 1963.

Native Plants of Pennsylvania. Washington Crossing, Pa.: Executive Committee for Bowman's Hill State Wild Flower Preserve, 1963.

Sperka, Marie, *Growing Wildflowers*. New York: Harper & Row, 1973.

Steffek, Edwin F. *Wild Flowers and How to Grow Them*. New York: Crown Publishers, 1954.

Stupka, Arthur. *Wildflowers in Color*. New York: Harper & Row, 1965.

Taylor, Kathryn S., and Stephen F. Hamblin, *Wild Flower Cultivation*. New York: Macmillan, 1963.

Wherry, Edgar T. *Wild Flower Guide*. New York: Doubleday, 1948.

Index

Passing references to plants are not indexed. Hundreds of common plant names have been cross-referenced for convenience, but in the three sections (sun, shade, moisture) where plants are described, the genera considered are listed alphabetically by the botanical names. In this index, common names beginning with words like false or wild are usually transposed so that they can be listed under the more meaningful part of the name: wolfsbane, wild. However, hyphenated common names are usually not transposed: trout-lily. Hybrids and named selections of various genera have not been indexed, but many now in commerce are described in the text.